Forensic Science Experiments

FACTS ON FILE SCIENCE EXPERIMENTS

Forensic Science Experiments

Pamela Walker
Elaine Wood

Facts On File
An imprint of Infobase Publishing

Forensic Science Experiments

Editor: Frank K. Darmstadt
Copy Editor for A Good Thing, Inc.: Betsy Feist
Project Coordination: Aaron Richman
Art Director: Howard Petlack
Production: Victoria Kessler
Illustrations: Hadel Studios

Facts On File, Inc.
An imprint of Infobase Publishing
132 West 31st Street
New York NY 10001

Library of Congress Cataloging-in-Publication Data
Walker, Pam, 1958-
Forensic science experiments/Pamela Walker, Elaine Wood.
p. cm.—(Facts on file, science experiments)
Includes bibliographical references and index.
ISBN 978-0-8160-7804-2 (acid-free paper)
1, Forensic sciences–Experiments. I. Wood, Elaine, 1950–   . Title.
HV8073.W332 2010
363.25–dc22
2008039900

Facts On File books are available at special discounts when purchased in bulk quantities for businesses, associations, institutions, or sales promotions. Please call our Special Sales Department in New York at 212/967-8800 or 800/322-8755.

You can find Facts On File on the World Wide Web at http://www.factsonfile.com

Cover printed by Bang Printing, Brainerd, MN
Book printed and bound by Bang Printing, Brainerd, MN
Date printed: July, 2010
Printed in the United States of America

10 9 8 7 6 5 4 3 2

This book is printed on acid-free paper.

Contents

Preface

For centuries, humans have studied and explored the natural world around them. The ever-growing body of knowledge resulting from these efforts is science. Information gained through science is passed from one generation to the next through an array of educational programs. One of the primary goals of every science education program is to help young people develop critical-thinking and problem-solving skills that they can use throughout their lives.

Science education is unique in academics in that it not only conveys facts and skills; it also cultivates curiosity and creativity. For this reason, science is an active process that cannot be fully conveyed by passive teaching techniques. The question for educators has always been, "What is the best way to teach science?" There is no simple answer to this question, but studies in education provide useful insights.

Research indicates that students need to be actively involved in science, learning it through experience. Science students are encouraged to go far beyond the textbook and to ask questions, consider novel ideas, form their own predictions, develop experiments or procedures, collect information, record results, analyze findings, and use a variety of resources to expand knowledge. In other words, students cannot just hear science; they must also do science.

"Doing" science means performing experiments. In the science curriculum, experiments play a number of educational roles. In some cases, hands-on activities serve as hooks to engage students and introduce new topics. For example, a discrepant event used as an introductory experiment encourages questions and inspires students to seek the answers behind their findings. Classroom investigations can also help expand information that was previously introduced or cement new knowledge. According to neuroscience, experiments and other types of hands-on learning help transfer new learning from short-term into long-term memory.

Facts On File Science Experiments is a six-volume set of experiments that helps engage students and enable them to "do" science. The high-interest experiments in these books put students' minds into gear and give them opportunities to become involved, to think independently, and to build on their own base of science knowledge.

As a resource, *Facts On File Science Experiments* provides teachers with new and innovative classroom investigations that are presented in a clear, easy-to-understand style. The areas of study in the six-volume set include forensic science, environmental science, computer research, physical science, weather and climate, and space and astronomy. Experiments are supported by colorful figures and line illustrations that help hold students' attention and explain information. All of the experiments in these books use multiple science process skills such as observing, measuring, classifying, analyzing, and predicting. In addition, some of the experiments require students to practice inquiry science by setting up and carrying out their own open-ended experiments.

Each volume of the set contains 20 new experiments as well as extensive safety guidelines, glossary, correlation to the National Science Education Standards, scope and sequence, and an annotated list of Internet resources. An introduction that presents background information begins each investigation to provide an overview of the topic. Every experiment also includes relevant specific safety tips along with materials list, procedure, analysis questions, explanation of the experiment, connections to real life, and an annotated further reading section for extended research.

Pam Walker and Elaine Wood, the authors of *Facts On File Science Experiments*, are sensitive to the needs of both science teachers and students. The writing team has more than 40 years of combined science teaching experience. Both are actively involved in planning and improving science curricula in their home state, Georgia, where Pam was the 2007 Teacher of the Year. Walker and Wood are master teachers who hold specialist degrees in science and science education. They are the authors of dozens of books for middle and high school science teachers and students.

Facts On File Science Experiments, by Walker and Wood, facilitates science instruction by making it easy for teachers to incorporate experimentation. During experiments, students reap benefits that are not available in other types of instruction. One of these benefits is the opportunity to take advantage of the learning provided by social interactions. Experiments are usually carried out in small groups, enabling students to brainstorm and learn from each other. The validity of group work as an effective learning tool is supported by research in neuroscience, which shows that the brain is a social organ and that communication and collaboration are activities that naturally enhance learning.

Experimentation addresses many different types of learning, including lateral thinking, multiple intelligences, and constructivism. In lateral thinking, students solve problems using nontraditional methods. Long-established, rigid procedures for problem-solving are replaced by original ideas from students. When encouraged to think laterally, students are more likely to come up with unique ideas that are not usually found in the traditional classroom. This type of thinking requires students to construct meaning from an activity and to think like scientists.

Another benefit of experimentation is that it accommodates students' multiple intelligences. According to the theory of multiple intelligences, students possess many different aptitudes, but in varying degrees. Some of these forms of intelligence include linguistic, musical, logical-mathematical, spatial, kinesthetic, intrapersonal, and interpersonal. Learning is more likely to be acquired and retained when more than one sense is involved. During an experiment, students of all intellectual types find roles in which they can excel.

Students in the science classroom become involved in active learning, constructing new ideas based on their current knowledge and their experimental findings. The constructivist theory of learning encourages students to discover principles for and by themselves. Through problem solving and independent thinking, students build on what they know, moving forward in a manner that makes learning real and lasting.

Active, experimental learning makes connections between newly acquired information and the real world, a world that includes jobs. In the twenty-first century, employers expect their employees to identify and solve problems for themselves. Therefore, today's students, workers of the near future, will be required to use higher-level thinking skills. Experience with science experiments provides potential workers with the ability and confidence to be problem solvers.

The goal of Walker and Wood in *Facts On File Science Experiments* is to provide experiments that hook and hold the interest of students, teach basic concepts of science, and help students develop their critical-thinking skills. When fully immersed in an experiment, students can experience those "Aha!" moments, the special times when new information merges with what is already known and understanding breaks through. On these occasions, real and lasting learning takes place. The authors hope that this set of books helps bring more "Aha" moments into every science class.

Acknowledgments

This book would not exist were it not for our editor, Frank K. Darmstadt, who conceived and directed the project. Frank supervised the material closely, editing and making invaluable comments along the way. Betsy Feist of A Good Thing, Inc., is responsible for transforming our raw material into a polished and grammatically correct manuscript that makes us proud.

Introduction

Almost everyone loves a good mystery, and mysteries are the meat of forensic science. The study of forensic science involves the analysis and interpretation of evidence for use in a court of law. Unlike "pure" disciplines, forensics is an applied science that uses scientific principles to meet specific goals. On the job, forensic scientists work to find out what happened at a crime scene. Such determinations are made by looking at the physical evidence at the scene and deducing what that evidence says about the crime. Many of the principles and techniques used by experts are incorporated into *Forensic Science Experiments*, one volume of the new *Facts On File Science Experiments* set. The goal of this volume is to share new, proven classroom experiments in forensic science with middle and high school teachers and students.

The use of forensics in the classroom is well-known to promote interest in science and to improve critical-thinking skills. Forensics is an engaging field of study, partly because of its popularization from media. The so-called "CSI effect," portrayal of the work of forensic scientists in crime-solving programs, has made students aware of the discipline. Although the depictions of television crime drama are not always completely accurate, they do reflect the use of science to solve problems. Such programming makes it clear to students that science is relevant in today's world.

For the teacher who wants to integrate various disciplines, forensic science is an ideal vehicle. This multidisciplinary field includes Earth science, physics, chemistry, biology, and anatomy and physiology. In the real-world work of forensics, these areas of study are not isolated, but strongly interrelated and interdependent.

Relying heavily on the scientific method, forensic science is inquiry based. Students are required to read, perform research, develop hypotheses, think analytically, and conduct interviews. Once their data is collected, students must analyze it, employ deductive reasoning, draw conclusions, and share their results with others. To carry out the experiments to solve these inquiries, forensics employs many standard laboratory techniques that require students to use equipment such as microscopes, glassware, balances, and hot plates.

In *Forensic Science Experiments*, we offer teachers and students 20 new science experiments that will provide a sound, interesting, and enjoyable introduction to forensic science. Experiments include several areas of the discipline. In "Banana Autopsy," students take on the roles of pathologists by carrying out examinations of "victims" of foul play, drawing conclusions about the cause of death, then sewing up the "bodies." "Characterization of Types of Carbohydrates" is a partial inquiry in which students develop protocols for distinguishing starch, cellulose, and glycogen. One of the full-inquiry experiments, "Rate of Cooling," asks students to design their own experiment to find out whether a body cools faster in air or in water. Other topics covered in this book include radioactive isotopes, shoes impressions, mitochondrial DNA, probative value of class evidence, DNA, blood spatter, specific gravity, soil identification, density, emission spectra of light, latent fingerprints, chromatography, deductive reasoning, presumptive blood test, lead poisoning, trace evidence, and textile fibers.

There is no better way to get students interested in a subject than to show them the usefulness of what they are studying. Through the participation in forensic science, students can have classroom experiences that help them see the connections between education and everyday life. Our hope is that once students are engaged in science, they will go on to build lifelong interests in the field.

Safety Precautions

REVIEW BEFORE STARTING ANY EXPERIMENT

Each experiment includes special safety precautions that are relevant to that particular project. These do not include all the basic safety precautions that are necessary whenever you are working on a scientific experiment. For this reason, it is absolutely necessary that you read and remain mindful of the General Safety Precautions that follow. Experimental science can be dangerous and good laboratory procedure always includes following basic safety rules. Things can happen quickly while you are performing an experiment—for example, materials can spill, break, or even catch on fire. There will not be time after the fact to protect yourself. Always prepare for unexpected dangers by following the basic safety guidelines during the entire experiment, whether or not something seems dangerous to you at a given moment.

We have been quite sparing in prescribing safety precautions for the individual experiments. For one reason, we want you to take very seriously the safety precautions that are printed in this book. If you see it written here, you can be sure that it is here because it is absolutely critical.

Read the safety precautions here and at the beginning of each experiment before performing each lab activity. It is difficult to remember a long set of general rules. By rereading these general precautions every time you set up an experiment, you will be reminding yourself that lab safety is critically important. In addition, use your good judgment and pay close attention when performing potentially dangerous procedures. Just because the book does not say "Be careful with hot liquids" or "Don't cut yourself with a knife" does not mean that you can be careless when boiling water or using a knife to punch holes in plastic bottles. Notes in the text are special precautions to which you must pay special attention.

GENERAL SAFETY PRECAUTIONS

Accidents can be caused by carelessness, haste, or insufficient knowledge. By practicing safety procedures and being alert while conducting experiments, you can avoid taking an unnecessary risk. Be sure to check the individual experiments in this book for additional safety regulations and adult supervision requirements. If you will be working in a laboratory, do not work alone. When you are working off site, keep in groups with a minimum of three students per group, and follow school rules and state legal requirements for the number of supervisors required. Ask an adult supervisor with basic training in first aid to carry a small first-aid kit. Make sure everyone knows where this person will be during the experiment.

PREPARING

- Clear all surfaces before beginning experiments.
- Read the entire experiment before you start.
- Know the hazards of the experiments and anticipate dangers.

PROTECTING YOURSELF

- Follow the directions step by step.
- Perform only one experiment at a time.
- Locate exits, fire blanket and extinguisher, master gas and electricity shut-offs, eyewash, and first-aid kit.
- Make sure there is adequate ventilation.
- Do not participate in horseplay.
- Do not wear open-toed shoes.
- Keep floor and workspace neat, clean, and dry.
- Clean up spills immediately.
- If glassware breaks, do not clean it up by yourself; ask for teacher assistance.
- Tie back long hair.
- Never eat, drink, or smoke in the laboratory or workspace.
- Do not eat or drink any substances tested unless expressly permitted to do so by a knowledgeable adult.

USING EQUIPMENT WITH CARE

- Set up apparatus far from the edge of the desk.
- Use knives or other sharp, pointed instruments with care.

- Pull plugs, not cords, when removing electrical plugs.
- Clean glassware before and after use.
- Check glassware for scratches, cracks, and sharp edges.
- Let your teacher know about broken glassware immediately.
- Do not use reflected sunlight to illuminate your microscope.
- Do not touch metal conductors.
- Take care when working with any form of electricity.
- Use alcohol-filled thermometers, not mercury-filled thermometers.

USING CHEMICALS

- Never taste or inhale chemicals.
- Label all bottles and apparatus containing chemicals.
- Read labels carefully.
- Avoid chemical contact with skin and eyes (wear safety glasses or goggles, lab apron, and gloves).
- Do not touch chemical solutions.
- Wash hands before and after using solutions.
- Wipe up spills thoroughly.

HEATING SUBSTANCES

- Wear safety glasses or goggles, apron, and gloves when heating materials.
- Keep your face away from test tubes and beakers.
- When heating substances in a test tube, avoid pointing the top of the test tube toward other people.
- Use test tubes, beakers, and other glassware made of Pyrex™ glass.
- Never leave apparatus unattended.
- Use safety tongs and heat-resistant gloves.
- If your laboratory does not have heatproof workbenches, put your Bunsen burner on a heatproof mat before lighting it.
- Take care when lighting your Bunsen burner; light it with the airhole closed and use a Bunsen burner lighter rather than wooden matches.

- Turn off hot plates, Bunsen burners, and gas when you are done.
- Keep flammable substances away from flames and other sources of heat.
- Have a fire extinguisher on hand.

FINISHING UP

- Thoroughly clean your work area and any glassware used.
- Wash your hands.
- Be careful not to return chemicals or contaminated reagents to the wrong containers.
- Do not dispose of materials in the sink unless instructed to do so.
- Clean up all residues and put in proper containers for disposal.
- Dispose of all chemicals according to all local, state, and federal laws.

BE SAFETY CONSCIOUS AT ALL TIMES!

1. Banana Autopsy

Topic

An autopsy can help determine cause of death.

Introduction

An *autopsy* or postmortem examination is a complete inspection of a corpse. Investigators often rely on an autopsy to help explain a decedent's cause and manner of death. *Pathologists* are specialized doctors who usually carry out autopsies. An autopsy is required when the cause of death is suspected to be a criminal matter or when the cause of death cannot be determined medically.

The first stage of an autopsy is an external exam of the body to search for trace evidence and to identify any wounds or markings. Next, the pathologist makes a Y incision from the shoulders to the chest, then down to the pubis. The rib cage above the heart and lungs is removed so that these and other organs can be taken out of the body, examined, and weighed. Stomach contents are also inspected to find out what was consumed last and at what time it was consumed. Samples of tissues from organs are preserved and body fluids are collected. A saw is used to open the back of the skull so that the brain can be examined. Once all internal regions have been studied, the chest and abdomen are stitched up, the skull is replaced, and the scalp is sewn back in place.

In this experiment, you will play the role of a forensic pathologist by carrying out a detailed autopsy to determine the cause of death.

Time Required

55 minutes

Materials

- teacher-prepared banana "victim"
- paper towels

- magnifying glass
- scalpel
- probe
- toothed forceps
- needle holder
- scissors
- sutures
- electronic scale or triple-beam balance
- tape measure or metric ruler
- science notebook

Safety Note   Take care when working with scalpels, needles, and other sharp objects. Please review and follow the safety guidelines at the beginning of this volume.

Procedure

1. If the name of the victim (examinee) is known, record it on the pathology report. Fill in the date and the name of the examining pathologist (you) on the report.

2. Carefully open the evidence sheet (paper towel) enclosing the victim.

3. Examine any materials in the evidence sheet or on the external surface of the clothing that may provide information about how this victim died. Use the magnifying glass to help you collect small pieces of trace evidence. Record you findings on the pathology report in the section labeled "Trace Evidence."

4. Remove the victim's clothing.

5. Exam the external surface of the victim. On the pathology report, note any birthmarks, scars, tattoos, or wounds. Measure these marks (in millimeters [mm]) and record the measurements on the report. Indicate the positions of these marks, scars, tattoos, or wounds on the diagram in the pathology report.

6. Weigh the victim and record the weight on the pathology report.

7. Measure and record the height of the victim.

8. Make a Y-shaped incision from the area of the shoulders to the mid-chest, then down to the pubic region (see Figure 1).

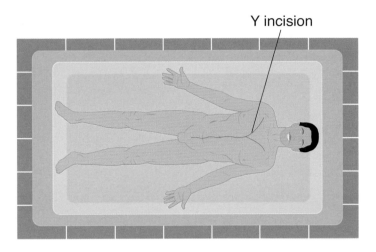

Y incision

Figure 1

9. Examine the victim internally. Record any evidence that can help you determine cause of death, such as damage to internal organs, bruising, bleeding, or wounds.

10. Examine the head externally and record your findings.

11. Using the scapel, make an incision across the back of the head, on the lower part of the skull from ear to ear. Open the skull and look for further evidence to indicate cause of death and record any findings.

12. Now that you have viewed the body externally and internally, suture the skull and the Y incision. To do so:

    a. Remove the curved needle with thread from the package. Gently tug on the thread to straighten it.

    b. Grasp the curved needle with the needle holder about two-thirds from the tip (see Figure 2).

    c. Gently use the toothed forceps to lift the edge of the skin farthest from you.

    d. Place the point of the needle against the exterior surface of the skin, about 5 to 10 mm (about 0.2 to 0.4 inches [in.]) from the incision.

    e. Rotate the wrist to pass the needle through the skin (from exterior surface to interior surface).

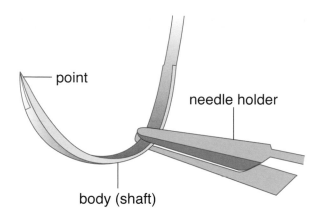

point

needle holder

body (shaft)

Figure 2

f. Release the needle and pick it up again on the inside of the skin. Rotate the wrist to work the needle completely through the skin. Release the skin from the toothed forceps.

g. Pick up the skin nearest you with the toothed forceps. Rotate the wrist to bring the needle through the skin (from interior surface to exterior surface).

h. Release the needle and pick it up again on the outside of the skin. Rotate the wrist to work the needle through the skin, leaving about a 5-centimeter (cm) (2-inch [in.]) "tail." Release the skin.

i. Tie a knot in the suture:

Loop the thread around the needle holder twice. With the needle holder, pick up the "tail" of the suture thread and pull it through the loops. (This makes the first part of the knot.) Gently tug on the suture thread to tighten. Repeat the process to finish the knot. (If you have trouble tying the knot with instruments, use your hands to tie a basic square knot in the thread.) Cut the thread.

j. Repeat steps a through i, using the same needle and thread until the entire incision is closed. If you need more thread, open another package.

Analysis

1. What type(s) of trace evidence did you find on the clothing of the victim?

2. How could trace evidence obtained during an autopsy be useful in solving a crime?

3. What kinds of marking(s) did you find on the skin of your victim?

4. How could markings on the skin such as scars or tattoos be useful in solving a crime?

5. What did you find when you opened the body cavity of the victim?

6. What did you find when you opened the skull of the victim?

7. Based on your findings, what was the cause of death?

8. Do you think it is likely that this victim's death is related to a crime? Explain your reasoning.

Pathology Report		
Name of examinee:	**Date:**	**Name of examiner:**
Trace Evidence:	Marks, scars, tattoos, or wounds and their positions: front back	
Weight:	Height:	
Chest and abdominal cavities:		
External examination of head:		
Internal examination of head:		

What's Going On?

During an autopsy, a pathologist has two goals: determine the manner of death and the cause of death. Manner of death falls into five categories: natural, accident, homicide, suicide, and undetermined. Cause of death refers to the injury, condition, or disease that led to death, such as puncture wound to the heart or heart failure due to heart attack.

A pathologist also tries to determine the time of death. In some cases, the time of death is very difficult to place and requires consideration of several factors. Therefore, pathologists rely on predictable changes that occur in the body after death to help estimate time of death. These changes include body temperature, *lividity, rigor,* and the stomach contents.

Body temperature drops at a predictable rate until it reaches air temperature. The rate at which body temperature falls depends on air temperature, wind, amount of clothing, and even the body weight of the deceased. "Lividity" refers to purplish areas that form on the body after the heart stops pumping and blood begins to settle. If a body is lying on its back at death, the back and hips develop regions of lividity. Rigor is a stiffening of the body that begins 2 to 6 hours after death, beginning at the neck and jaw. After 24 to 80 hours (depending on the environment), rigor ends and the muscles begin to relax. Examination of the gastric (stomach and intestinal) contents and their location in the digestive tract helps the pathologist decide when the last meal was eaten. All of this evidence taken together can reveal a picture that helps establish time of death.

Connections

Autopsy findings can be critical in determining cause of death. Trace evidence on the body such as human or pet hair; fibers from clothing, carpets, or cars; and soil or dust particles can indicate where a victim was located at the time of death. Injuries to the body may also help establish what caused death. Examination of organs can tell a pathologist whether death occurred from natural causes or whether foul play was involved. For example, narrowing of blood vessels around the heart and blood clots in lungs tell the examiner that the victim died from disease. Blood inside the skull may indicate a head injury. Damage to the *hyoid* bone, a small structure in the neck, can be an indication of strangulation. By assessing all of the clues found during autopsy, a pathologist can often determine the events that occurred in the last few hours of a person's life.

Want to Know More?

See appendix for Our Findings.

Further Reading

Friedlander, E.R. *Autopsy*, 1999. The Pathology Guy. Available online. URL: http://www.pathguy.com/autopsy.htm. Accessed May 7, 2008. Written by Dr. Ed Friedlander, this Web site explains autopsy procedures and includes helpful animations.

Valdes, Robert. "Autopsies," How Stuff Works. Available online. URL: http://health.howstuffworks.com/autopsy.htm. Accessed May 7, 2008. This Web site explains the basics of autopsies in layman's terms.

Verma, Ajay Mark. "Virtual Autopsies," University of Leicester. Available online. URL: http://www.le.ac.uk/pa/tach/va/titlpag1.html. Accessed May 7, 2008. This Web site includes 18 cases, along with interactive information to help students analyze information provided during an autopsy.

2. Characterization of Types of Carbohydrates

Topic

Glycogen, cellulose, and starch can be differentiated by chemical tests.

Introduction

You are working for a forensic laboratory that has lost all its records in a fire. The lab is trying to reestablish its protocols for identifying different materials. You have been asked to determine which kinds of chemical tests can be used to identify three carbohydrates: *starch, cellulose,* and *glycogen*. Starch and cellulose are both found in plants. Glycogen is a carbohydrate found in animals. The ability to identify these carbohydrates could help distinguish a sample of plant tissue from one of animal tissue.

You already know something about these substances. Carbohydrates are complex molecules made from long chains of glucose. Plants make the starch to store glucose molecules. Starch is a soft, pliable compound that is found inside roots and fruits. Plants also manufacture cellulose, another glucose polymer, which differs structurally and functionally from starch. Whereas starch is flexible and soft, cellulose is stiff and serves as a structural component of plant cells. (Cellulose is the molecule that gives wood its strength.) Glycogen is a form of starch that is manufactured in animal cells. Like plant starch, glycogen is relatively soft and serves as a reservoir for glucose molecules.

The forensics lab needs a procedure, or a set of tests, to differentiate these three carbohydrates. Your job is to determine how these three molecules respond to different chemical tests. The chemical tests you will perform are: reaction to iodine, solubility in hot water, and digestion in amylase. Once you complete the tests, you will write a procedure explaining how the lab can differentiate these types of carbohydrates.

 **Time Required**

90 minutes

Materials

- powdered starch (about 1 teaspoon [tsp])
- powdered cellulose (about 1 tsp)
- powdered glycogen (about 1 tsp)
- distilled water (about 50 milliliters [ml] for making solutions)
- access to water
- iodine (or Lugol's) solution
- Benedict's solution
- amylase solution
- spatula
- hot plate
- 250-ml beaker
- 3 test tubes
- test-tube rack
- test-tube holder
- pipettes
- test-tube brush
- test-tube clamp
- 3 labels
- science notebook

Safety Note Wear protective goggles when working with chemicals. Be careful when working with hot plates and hot water. Please review and follow the safety guidelines at the beginning of this volume.

Procedure

1. Test the three carbohydrates with iodine to see how each reacts. To do so:

    a. Label three test tubes as "starch," "cellulose," and "glycogen."

b. Fill each test tube about one-quarter full of distilled water.

c. Add a half spatula of the appropriate powder to each test tube. Shake gently to mix.

d. Add a few drops of iodine solution to each test tube. Shake gently to mix. Observe the colors in each test tube and record your observations on Data Table 1.

e. Clean your test tubes.

2. Test the three carbohydrates to see which one(s) dissolves in hot water. To do so:

a. Place a half spatula of each carbohydrate in the appropriate test tube.

b. Add a few drops of distilled water to each test tube and swirl gently to mix.

c. Heat the test tubes in a boiling water bath for 5 minutes.

d. Use a test-tube clamp to carefully remove each test tube from the water and place in the test-tube rack. Observe the test tubes to see if the carbohydrate powders are dissolved. Record you observations on Data Table 1.

3. When the tubes are cool, check the carbohydrates in each to see which ones can be digested by amylase. To do so:

a. Add one drop of pancreatic amylase solution to each test tube.

b. Let the test tubes sit for 15 minutes.

c. When a carbohydrate is digested, it forms sugar. Test the contents of each tube with Benedict's solution for the presence of sugar. To do so:

i. Pour 5 ml of Benedict's solution into each test tube. Gently shake each test tube to mix.

ii. Heat the test tubes in a beaker of boiling water for 3 minutes.

iii. Use a test-tube holder to carefully remove the test tubes from the water and place them in the test-tube rack. Allow the test tubes to cool.

iv. Observe the test tubes. The formation of a green, red, or yellow color is a positive test for the presence of simple sugar. In Figure 1, the test-tube on the left is a positive Benedict's test. Record you test results on Data Table 1.

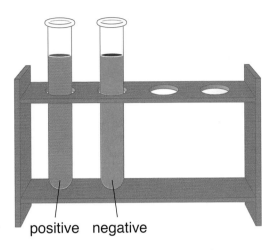

positive   negative

Figure 1

Data Table 1			
Type of carbohydrate	Reaction to iodine	Solubility in hot water	Digestion by amylase (per Benedict's test)
Starch			
Cellulose			
Glycogen			

Analysis

1. Describe the reaction of each carbohydrate to iodine.

2. Which carbohydrate(s) dissolved in hot water?

3. Which carbohydrate(s) were digested by amylase?

4. Write a detailed lab procedures on Data Table 2 to positively identify each of the three carbohydrates. (*Hint:* A lab procedure is a set of instructions explaining what to do in the lab.)

Data Table 2
Lab procedure to identify starch:
Lab procedure to identify cellulose:
Lab procedure to identify glycogen:

What's Going On?

All carbohydrates are biologically important molecules made from chains of glucose. Despite their similarities, each type of carbohydrate has distinctive chemical properties. Chemical tests can be used to help differentiate carbohydrates. Two of the tests in this experiment yield a color change.

In the iodine (Lugol's) test, a few drop of iodine solution are added to a sample of carbohydrate. Starch turns blue-black in the presence of iodine. Glycogen turns brown-blue. Cellulose does not respond to iodine, so remains the brown-yellow color of the reagent.

The Benedict's test yields a yellow, red, or green color that is a positive test for the presence of glucose and other simple sugars. Starch and glycogen are digested by the enzyme amylase into simple sugars, so they yield a positive Benedict's test. In the solubility test, a visual examination of the carbohydrate shows whether or not it dissolves in hot water. Starch and glycogen dissolve, but cellulose does not. Used together, these three tests can show whether a sample of tissue containing carbohydrate is from plant or animal origin.

Connections

The job of a forensic scientist is to find ways to solve problems, identify materials, and find out where the materials originated. Materials can be analyzed through chemical tests to determine if they are of plant or animal origin. To ensure accuracy, labs providing chemical analyses for forensic investigations must develop and follow specific guidelines for conducting chemical tests.

Tests conducted in forensic labs help solve crimes. In one case, a forensic lab was asked to examine the stomach contents of a homicide victim to see if anything could be learned about the victim's activities just before death. Chemical tests, including the iodine test, the Benedict's test, and the pancreatic amylase test, demonstrated that the victim's stomach contained a lot of starch.

This evidence suggested to investigators that the victim might have recently eaten a baked potato, which was a specialty of his favorite restaurant. At the restaurant, other diners and the wait staff did indeed remember seeing the victim and were able to describe his dinner guest. This information, coupled with other work done by investigators, helped lead police to the murderer.

 Want to Know More?

See appendix for Our Findings.

Further Reading

Carpi, Anthony. "Carbohydrates," Visionlearning. Available online. URL: http://www.visionlearning.com/library/module_viewer.php?mid=61. Accessed May 10, 2008. Supported by the National Science Foundation and U.S. Department of Education, this Web site provides excellent information on organic compounds.

Farabee, Michael J. *Online Biology Book*, Macicopan, September 2006. Available online. URL: http://www.emc.maricopa.edu/faculty/farabee/BIOBK/BioBookTOC.html. Accessed May 10, 2008. Hosted by Estsrella Mountain Community College, Avondale, Arizona, the *Online Biology Book* provides information on organic compounds and other topics in biology.

Hoffman, Brian. "Carbohydrates, Quantitative Tests." Available online. URL: http://apple.cmu.edu.tw/~a001003/Carbohydrates%20-%20 Qualitative%20Tests.htm. Accessed May 10, 2008. This Web site, which is supported by Park University, Parkville, Missouri, explains the science behind several chemical tests on carbohydrates.

3. Techniques in Making Shoe Impressions

Topic

Crime scene investigators make shoe impressions with plaster of paris and dental stone.

Introduction

The most common method of entering and leaving an area where a crime is committed is by walking. Criminalists often gain information by examining the surfaces on which a perpetrator walked. Footwear or bare feet can leave superficial prints on firm surfaces such as flooring. However, walking across a soft surface like damp soil leaves impressions or indentations.

Footwear impressions can provide crucial clues in an investigation. Prints or impressions can show the points of entry and exit at the crime scene. In addition, shoes carry materials from one environment to another. This material can provide information about where this person has been.

An impression can tell a lot about the shoe that made it. Every shoe is unique, with its own pattern of wear and tear. Therefore an impression of footwear can be compared to a particular pair of shoes to help connect those shoes to the crime scene. Impressions can also tell something about the height and weight of the wearer. Heavy individuals make deeper impressions than light ones. In addition, a tall person has a longer stride than a short person.

There are several techniques for making casts of shoe impressions. In this experiment, you will compare the effectiveness of two materials in making casts: plaster of paris and dental stone.

 Time Required

45 minutes on day 1
45 minutes on day 2

Materials

- 2 pounds (lbs)(0.91 kilograms [kg]) of dental stone in a large Ziploc™ bag

- 3 lbs (1.36 kg) of plaster of paris in a large ziplock bag

- 3 to 5 cups of water in a bottle

- 5 to 10 twigs or craft (Popsicle™) sticks soaked in water

- 3 or 4 long strips of cardboard (about 4 inches [in.] by 24 in. [10.2 centimeters (cm) by 61 cm])

- large spoon

- talcum powder

- magnifying glass

- scrub brush

- paper towels

- access to water

- science notebook

Safety Note   Please review and follow the safety guidelines at the beginning of this volume.

Procedure, Day 1

1. Follow your teacher to an outdoor area where there are some shoe impressions.

2. Closely examine two footprints. Carefully remove any rocks, twigs, or other debris from the footprints.

3. Sprinkle a little talcum powder over these two footprints to help hold the soil in place and secure the impressions.

4. Build a retaining wall around each impression using strips of cardboard (see Figure 1). (This wall will prevent the plaster of paris or dental stone from escaping when it is poured into the impression.)

5. Make a cast of one footprint using dental stone. To do so:

   a. Pour about 1 cup of water into the Ziploc™ bag of dental stone.

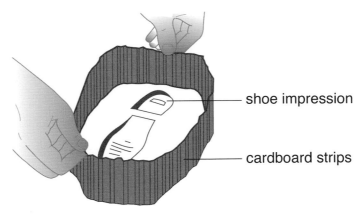

shoe impression

cardboard strips

Figure 1

b. Knead the bag of dental stone for 2 to 3 minutes (min) to mix thoroughly.

c. Examine the consistency of the dental stone. Ideally, it should be similar to pancake batter. If it is too thick, add a little more water. (Be careful; if you add too much water, your mixture will be too thin.)

d. The dental stone becomes firm very quickly, so work rapidly to pour the mixture. Avoid pouring the material directly into the impression, which can distort it. Instead, hold the spoon just above the impression and slowly pour the mixture into the spoon so that it falls into the impression. When the impression is about half full, remove the spoon and pour the remaining mixture directly. The poured cast should be 2 to 3 in. (about 5 to 7.5 cm) thick.

e. Use a stick or pencil to etch your name and the date in the upper surface of dental stone.

f. Let the cast sit for 30 min to harden. During this time, carry out step 6 below.

g. After 30 min or more, insert the handle of the spoon into the ground about 1/2 in. (1.2 cm) from the impression and gently pry up the cast.

h. The cast may have soil or grass on it; do not remove it at this time.

i. Take the cast indoors and allow it to harden for 24 hours.

6. Make a cast of the other shoe impression using plaster of paris. To do so:

    a. Pour about 1 cup of water into the Ziploc™ bag of plaster of paris.

    b. Knead the bag of plaster of paris and water for 2 to 3 min to mix thoroughly.

    c. Examine the consistency of the mixture. Ideally, it should be similar to pancake batter. If it is too thick, add a little more water. (Be careful; if you add too much water, your mixture will be too thin.)

    d. Pour about 1/2 in. (1.2 cm) of plaster of paris into the impression, using the spoon as you did earlier to avoid damaging the impression. Add some reinforcing materials such as twigs or craft (Popsicle™) sticks that have been soaked in water (see Figure 2). (Dry sticks will absorb water from the plaster of paris and make it brittle.) Quickly finish pouring the plaster of paris into the impression to a thickness of at least 3 in.

    e. Follow directions e through i in step 5.

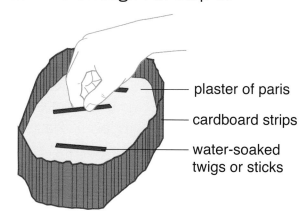

plaster of paris

cardboard strips

water-soaked twigs or sticks

Figure 2

Procedure, Day 2

1. Examine each shoe cast. In your science notebook, note any significant differences in the casts.

2. Using a scrub brush, gently clean each cast with water. Pat dry each cast with paper towels.

3. Examine each shoe cast again. In your notebook, note whether or not washing damaged either cast.

4. Closely examine each shoe cast with a magnifying glass. Search for nicks, cuts, or scrapes in the casts that indicate identifying markings on the shoes. Record these in your science notebook.

Analysis

1. Why might an investigator make casts of shoe impressions?
2. In your opinion, which cast was easier to pour, the dental stone or plaster of paris? Explain your answer.
3. Which material held up best to washing? Explain your answer.
4. Which material provided the most detail when viewed under the magnifying glass? Explain your answer.
5. Describe any nicks, scratches, wear patterns, or other unique marks found in either cast.
6. What information might a forensic investigator acquire from examining a shoe cast?
7. Complete a Venn diagram (see Figure 3) comparing the two casting materials.

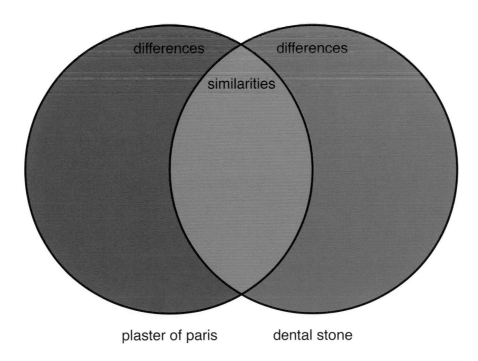

Figure 3

What's Going On?

Ideally, footprints at a crime scene can lead investigators to the person who made them. A clear shoe impression can yield a distinctive and easy-to-read cast. The quality of impressions varies with weather conditions, amount of moisture in the soil, and the type of soil. Clay-based soils, which are fine-grained and sticky, produce better impressions than sand, a loose soil made of relatively large grains.

For investigators, there are many benefits to taking a cast. Casts provide lifelike, actual-size molds of prints. Close examination of a cast can reveal microscopic nicks and scratches on the shoe as well as unique patterns of wear.

Connections

In the past, plaster of paris was the most commonly used material for making casts. Now, dental stone is generally recommended. Dental stone is harder than plaster, is more durable, and gives finer impressions. In addition, it does not have to be supported by reinforcing material and it lasts longer. With few exceptions, dental stone is the first choice of crime scene investigators working in the field.

 ## Want to Know More?

See appendix for Our Findings.

Further Reading

clt.uwa.edu. "Forensic Investigations, Impressions" Australian School Innovation in Science, Technology and Mathematics. Available online. URL: http://www.clt.uwa.edu.au/__data/page/112506/fsp08_impressions. pdf. Access May 11, 2008. This Web site provides an excellent explanation of the importance of impressions and the casts they yield.

Hilderbrand, Dwayne S. "Footwear, the Missed Evidence." Available online. URL: http://www.crimeandclues.com/footwear.htm. Accessed May 11, 2008. Hilderbrand, of the Scottsdale Police Crime Lab, Scottsdale, Arizona, discusses techniques in making shoe impressions.

SweetHaven. "Casts and Molds." *Crime Scene Investigation*, 2006. Available online. URL: http://www.free-ed.net/sweethaven/CrimeJustice/ CSI/default.asp?iNum=08. Accessed May 11, 2008. This excellent guide to making casts of footprints and tire tracks includes diagrams and drawings to enhance explanations.

4. Dating With Radioactive Isotopes

Topic

Radioactive isotopes decay at a steady rate, making them useful in dating bones and other remains.

Introduction

Determining the date of death of a deceased person has always been an important part of a criminal investigation. Scientists have primarily relied on the rate of decomposition to help them set this date. However, the rate at which tissue decomposes varies with temperature and moisture. New research has provided a more reliable method, one based on *radioactive isotopes* in the bones.

Bones and all other types of matter are composed of atoms. The nucleus of an atom is made up of two components: protons and neutrons. All the atoms of a given element have the same number of protons in their nuclei, but the number of neutrons can vary. Elements with the same number of protons but different number of neutrons are *isotopes*. Radioactive isotopes, atoms with unstable nuclei, break down at a constant rate. As they decay, the atoms release energy and subatomic particles as parent material changes into a more stable form called the "daughter" element. The time it takes for half of the parent isotope to break down into daughter material is known as *half-life.* Figure 1 shows the relationship of the percentage of parent material to the length of time that passes. By comparing the percentage of parent element to daughter element, one can determine the age of a sample. In this laboratory, a piece of string represents a radioactive isotope. You will examine the way isotopes break down through radioactive decay.

Time Required

55 minutes

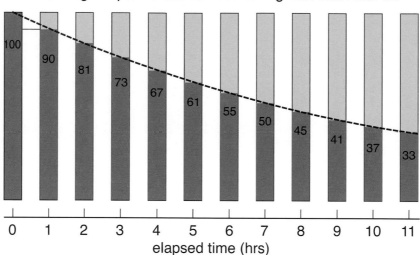

Percentage of parent element remaining with each half-life

Figure 1

Materials

- piece of string (about 40 inches [in.] [101.6 centimeters (cm)])
- ruler
- graph paper
- science notebook

Safety Note   Please review and follow the safety guidelines at the beginning of this volume.

Procedure

1. Copy the data table in your science notebook.

2. Measure the length of the piece of string. Record the length on the data table in the row labeled "Start." The length of this string represents the life of a radioactive isotope.

3. Cut the string in half and discard one of the halves. Measure the remaining length of string and record its length in the row labeled "After one half-life." This length of string represents the first half-life of the string.

4. Repeat step 3 until you can no longer cut the string in half. After each cut, record the length of the string in the appropriate row of the data table. If necessary, extend the data table to accommodate your measurements.

Data Table	
	Length of string
Start	
After one half-life	
After two half-lives	
After three half-lives	
After four half-lives	
After five half-lives	

5. Draw a line graph of the data you have collected on your data table. Place "Half-life" on the X-axis and "Length of string" on the Y-axis.

Analysis

1. Describe the shape of your graph.

2. How many half-lives did this string, which represents a radioactive element, undergo?

3. Why did you stop cutting the string in half?

4. Did the string ever disappear?

5. If you were given 20 grams (g) of a radioactive isotope, how many grams of the material would remain after three half-lives?

6. If the half-life of the radioactive isotope in question 5 is 50 days, how many days have passed in three half-lives?

7. If you had 50 g of a radioactive isotope whose half-life is 8 hours, how many grams of the material would remain after 32 hours?

8. How can scientists use radioactive isotopes to help determine the age of human remains?

What's Going On?

Carbon-14 (C-14) is a radioactive isotope that scientists use to calculate the age of rocks and very old archeological items. For such old materials, C-14 is useful because this isotope has a half-life of 5,700 years. After one half-life, or 5,700 years, half of the radioactive isotope in a sample of material decays. However, C-14 is not very helpful in pinpointing the ages of human remains. Recently, forensic scientists have been using radioisotopes with short half-lives: lead-210, with a half-life of 22 years, and polonium-210, whose half-life is just 138 days. These two isotopes are found in the natural environment.

A living body takes in elements, along with their natural radioactive isotopes. For example, lead-210 is present in our food, and it accumulates in the body during a person's life. Once people die, their bodies no longer take in the isotope. Every 138 days, half of the lead in the body decays, or breaks down, into another element. After twice that time, 276 days, three-fourths of the isotope is gone. Calculating the amount of isotope remaining in the bones enables scientists to pinpoint the time of death within a year.

Connections

The use of radioisotopes to date bones in forensic cases is new. In addition to lead-210 and polonium-210, other isotopes are also proving useful. Natural isotopes of hydrogen and oxygen, the two components of water, vary from one geographical location to another. These elements and others can be used to help determine the origin of remains. Forensic labs often analyze the ratio of these isotopes in hair, which grows about 0.4 in. (1 cm) a month. Analysis of isotopes in hair can show where a victim has lived in the last few months of his or her life. This information can be helpful in establishing the identity of unknown remains.

Want to Know More?

See appendix for Our Findings.

Further Reading

BBC.co.uk. "Physics Radioactivity." Available online. URL: http://www.bbc.co.uk/schools/gcsebitesize/physics/radioactivity/radioactivedecayandhalfliferev1.shtml. Accessed May 11, 2008. Maintained by the BBC, this Web site supports all areas of education, including the topic of radioactivity.

Brain, Marshall. "How Carbon-14 Dating Works." How Stuff Works. Available online. URL: http"//science.howstuffworks.com/carbon-142.htm. Accessed May 11, 2008. The chemistry behind radioactive decay is explained in layman's terms.

University of Colorado. "Half-life," *Physics 2000*. Available online. URL: http://www.colorado.edu/physics/2000/isotopes/radioactive_decay3.html. Accessed May 11, 2008. Created by the department of physics at the University of Colorado, this Web site provides information on radioactivity.

5. Mitochondrial DNA

Topic

Mitochondrial DNA can be used to help identify unknown remains.

Introduction

DNA is the genetic material in cells. Most of a cell's DNA is found in the nucleus. However, *mitochondria*, the *organelles* that convert glucose into energy, also contain a small amount of DNA. An individual's mitochondrial DNA is inherited from his or her mother only. The reason for this is found in the way sperm and egg cells are formed.

In the world of cells, eggs are huge. They contain a nucleus with its DNA as well as a large amount of cytoplasm and organelles. Sperm are small, streamlined cells that have shed all of their cytoplasm to enable them to swim quickly and efficiently toward the egg. A sperm's DNA is located in the head of the cell (see Figure 1), and its mitochondria are wrapped around the midsection. When a sperm and egg join, only the head of the sperm enters the maternal cell. The rest of the sperm, including the tail and the midpiece with its mitochondria, breaks off and falls away.

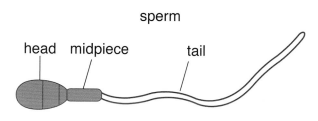

sperm

head   midpiece   tail

Figure 1

Mitochondrial DNA (mtDNA) is much smaller than nuclear DNA, measuring only about 16,500 base pairs in length. Nuclear DNA (nDNA), on the other hand, is made up of 3 billion base pairs. Geneticists use mtDNA to link individuals to family members.

Mitochondrial DNA is especially useful in analyzing old, highly decayed remains. Over time, soft tissue such as muscle, skin, and fat, breaks down and does not offer any material for genetic analysis. Tissue that degrades slowly, such as hair, bone, and teeth, is often all that forensic scientists have with which to work. While a cell only contains two copies of nDNA (one from each parent), it holds hundreds of mitochondria, each containing mtDNA. Within cells, this mtDNA is well protected and survives longer than nDNA. In cases where the amount of nDNA is limited, mtDNA can prove extremely useful.

In this experiment, you have been assigned a cold case. Bianca is a young woman who has been missing for a year. Hikers have recently found the skeletal remains of a person at the base of a steep cliff. From examination of the bones, the medical examiner states that these remains belong to a female between the ages of 18 and 33. The examiner also points out that the person probably died about one year ago. You will evaluate information from mtDNA analysis to help determine if the remains could be those of Bianca.

Time Required

55 minutes

Materials

•⦾ science notebook

Safety Note   Please review and follow the safety guidelines at the beginning of this volume.

Procedure, Part A

1. Examine the base sequence from a section of mtDNA obtained from remains to the sequence of bases from members of Bianca's family, her brother, sister, mother, and father.

Skeletal remains	**TACTACCCCAAAGGATACGATTCC**
Brother	TACTACCCCAAAGGATACGATTCC
Sister	TACTACCCCAAAGGATACGATTCC
Mother	TACTACCCCAAAGGATACGATTCC
Father	TACTACCCAACCGGATACGATTCC

2. Notice any similarities or differences in these sequences. Record your observations in your science notebook.

Procedure, Part B

1. Examine the pedigree in Figure 2 that shows the inheritance of a particular sequence of DNA. On a pedigree, circles represent females and squares represent males. If an individual shows a particular trait or genetic sequence, the square or circle is filled in. The line between a square and a circle indicates a union. Children of a union are shown just below the couple.

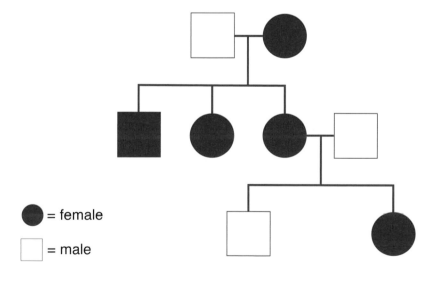

● = female

□ = male

Figure 2

2. Make notes about the pattern(s) of inheritance of this sequence of DNA in your science notebook. Use your notes to help you answer the Analysis questions.

Analysis

1. In part A of the procedure:
   a. How do the mtDNA sequences of the remains compare to Bianca's brother?
   b. How do the mtDNA sequences of the remains compare to Bianca's sister?
   c. How do the mtDNA sequences of the remains compare to Bianca's mother?
   d. How do the mtDNA sequences of the remains compare to Bianca's father?
2. Based on what you know about the inheritance of mtDNA, write the mtDNA sequence for Bianca's maternal aunt (her mother's sister).
3. Name another family member who could not be used to help identify Bianca's mtDNA.
4. In part B of the procedure, you examined the pedigree in Figure 2.
   a. In this pedigree, which parent carries the trait or genetic sequence that we are interested in examining?
   b. There are three children from the union of this couple. Who carries the genetic sequence of interest, the son, the daughters, or all three children?
   c. Based on your analysis of this pedigree, does this show the inheritance of a genetic sequence through nuclear DNA or mtDNA?
5. The pedigree in Figure 3 is not complete. Fill in this pedigree by darkening the correct circles and squares to show the inheritance of the sequence of interest in Bianca's family. Bianca is represented by the filled-in circle.
6. Do males pass on their mtDNA? Why or why not?

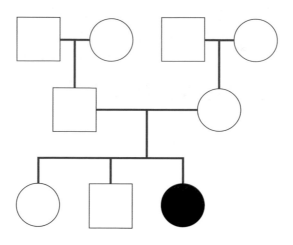

Figure 3

7. A grave has been discovered that may be the grave of Suzanne's great-great-grandmother, Clara. Suzanne's entire family has agreed to donate cells for the testing of mtDNA to determine if the woman in the grave is Clara. To save time and money, Suzanne studies the family pedigree. On the pedigree, Suzanne is indicated with a white circle that contains black dots and Clara is shown with a black circle that contains white dots. Suzanne identifies only nine family members (excluding herself) who need to be tested. Locate the squares or circles for those nine family members on the pedigree (Figure 4) and fill them in with pen or pencil.

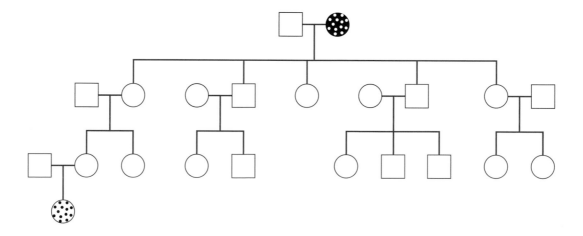

Figure 4

What's Going On?

Cells of plants and animals can be divided into two distinct regions. The nucleus is the reservoir of most of the cell's genetic information. The cytoplasm makes up the rest of the cell and it is filled with organelles. One type of organelle, the mitochondria, is unique because it contains its own DNA. Compared to nuclear DNA, mtDNA is very small, coding for only a few short proteins.

Since offspring only inherit mitochondria from their mothers, mtDNA can be used to link unknown remains to certain families. A mother and her children have mtDNA with either exactly the same, or extremely similar, nucleotide sequences. Therefore, if investigators suspect that the skeletal remains belong to a certain individual, they can ask that person's mother, maternal aunt, maternal grandmother, or children to give blood samples for mtDNA testing. The father's mtDNA cannot be used because children do not inherit mtDNA through paternal lines.

Connections

In some cases, hair and hair fragments are the only pieces of biological evidence found at a crime scene. The cells that make up the shaft of a hair are dead and do not contain nuclear DNA. If a hair's root is still attached, nuclear DNA can be extracted from root cells.

However, the dead cells making up the shaft of a hair still contain mtDNA. In one case, a seven-year-old girl was kidnapped from her home and murdered. Police suspected that the perpetrator was the girl's neighbor, but they had no proof. A search of the neighbor's home produced some dog hairs, which was peculiar since the man did not own a dog. However, the victim's family did have a dog. Hairs that are shed by dogs do not have hair roots attached to them, so they cannot yield nuclear DNA. Despite this problem, the forensic lab was able to analyze the mtDNA from the hairs to provide a match that helped convict the neighbor.

 Want to Know More?

See appendix for Our Findings.

Further Reading

Isenberg, Alice R. "Mitochondrial DNA Analysis at the FBI Laboratory." *Forensic Science Communications*, Volume 1, Number 2, July 1999. Available online. URL: http://www.fbi.gov/hq/lab/fsc/backissu/july1999/dnatext.htm#Back%20to%20text,%20Figure%201. Accessed May 11, 2008. This Web site, supported by the Department of Justice, offers an excellent explanation of the value of mtDNA in forensic work.

Kirsch, Laura. "Heating Up Cold Cases: Unsolved." *The Forensic Examiner,* June 22, 2006. Available online. URL: http://www.encyclopedia.com/doc/1G1-147201411.html. Accessed May 11, 2008. On this Web site, Kirsch explains the roles of various types of DNA samples in solving cold cases.

Sykes, Bryan. "Mitochondrial DNA and Human History," *The Human Genome*, October 10, 2003. Available online. URL: http://genome.wellcome.ac.uk/doc_WTD020876.html. Accessed May 11, 2008. Authored by Bryan Sykes, professor of human genetics at the Weatherall Institute of Molecular Medicine, University of Oxford, this Web site offers a clear and concise explanation of the value of mtDNA.

6. Gel Electrophoresis in DNA Fingerprinting

Topic

Gel electrophoresis is one phase in the production of a DNA fingerprint.

Introduction

DNA, or deoxyribonucleic acid, is the carrier of genetic information. This long molecule, found in the nuclei of almost all cells, is comprised of thousands of *nucleotides*, individual units each of which contains a nitrogen base, a sugar, and a phosphate group. Every DNA molecule is made up of two strands of nucleotides that are twisted around each other to form a double helix (see Figure 1). The order in which nucleotides are arranged in a strand of DNA is unique to each individual, very much like a fingerprint is unique. For this reason, *DNA fingerprints* can be used to identify individuals.

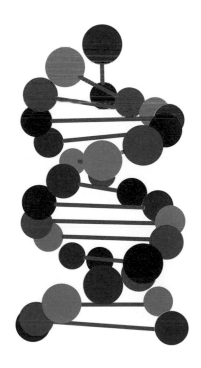

Figure 1

DNA double helix

To create a DNA fingerprint, scientists first cut the long molecule into shorter segments with restriction enzymes. The DNA segments are then separated by size on an agarose gel in the process of *gel electrophoresis*. There is only a very slim chance that the arrangement of DNA segments produced in this way will be the same for any two individuals. In this experiment, you will carry out the process of gel electrophoresis.

Time Required

two 55 minute periods

Materials

- 0.4 grams (g) agarose powder
- 5 milliliters (ml) concentrated buffer solution
- 250 ml distilled water
- 150-ml beaker
- 250-ml beaker
- graduated cylinder
- thermometer
- electronic scale or triple-beam balance
- hot plate
- hot mitts
- precut, dyed DNA samples (about 2 ml)
- micropipette
- pipettes
- stirring rod
- electrophoresis chamber with tray and comb
- electrode leads
- DC power supply
- masking tape
- science notebook

Procedure

1. Prepare the agarose gel. To do so:
   a. Use the electronic scale or triple-beam balance to measure 0.4 g powdered agarose. Pour the powdered agarose in the 150-ml beaker.
   b. Add 1 ml of buffer solution to the beaker.
   c. Add 50 ml of distilled water to the beaker. Gently stir the buffer, water, and agarose.
   d. Gently heat the beaker on the hot plate until the solution is clear.
   e. Turn off the hot plate and use hot mitts to remove the beaker to a heat-proof surface. Place the thermometer in the beaker.

2. Stretch a piece of masking tape across each open end of the electrophoresis tray. Be sure that the tape makes a tight seal so that agarose will not escape.

3. Stand the comb in the electrophoresis tray, positioning the sides of the comb in the tray's slots. Use tape to secure the ends of the comb to the tray.

4. When the solution in the beaker has cooled to 131 degrees Fahrenheit (°F) (55 degrees Celsius [°C]), collect a few ml of gel in the pipette. Run a bead of gel along the interface of the gel chamber and the tape to improve the seal between the tape and chamber.

5. Give the bead of gel a minute to solidify then gently pour the cooled solution into the electrophoresis tray until the gel comes halfway up the teeth of the comb (see Figure 2).

6. Allow the gel to set. This will take 10 to 15 minutes. As the gel solidifies, it becomes cloudy.

7. Carefully remove the tape on the ends of the tray and the tape that holds the comb in place in the electrophoresis tray. Remove the comb from the gel and set it aside. Notice that the comb left a row of holes or wells in the gel.

8. Place the electrophoresis tray with the gel into the electrophoresis chamber.

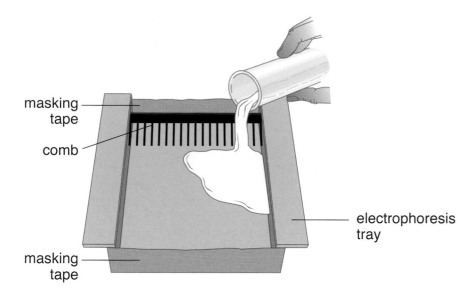

masking tape

comb

masking tape

electrophoresis tray

Figure 2

9. Prepare a dilute solution of buffer. To do so:

    a. Pour 4 ml of concentrated buffer into the 250-ml beaker.

    b. Add 196 ml of distilled water. Gently stir.

10. Pour the dilute solution of buffer over the gel in the electrophoresis chamber.

11. Use the micropipette to collect a small amount of one of the DNA samples. Carefully insert the tip of the pipette beneath the buffer and into one of the wells. Do not push the pipette through the walls of the well. Gently squeeze the bulb to force a few drops of DNA into the well (see Figure 3).

12. Repeat step 6 with the other DNA samples, inserting each sample into a different well with a clean micropipette tip.

13. Cover the electrophoresis chamber with a lid. Connect the electrophoresis chamber to the power supply with electrode leads.

14. Set the voltage to 100 volts (see Figure 4). Let the power run for from 45 minutes to 2 hours, or until the DNA samples reach the end of the gel.

15. Turn off the power. Remove the gel electrophoresis tray. Examine the patterns of DNA fragments that are visible on the gel.

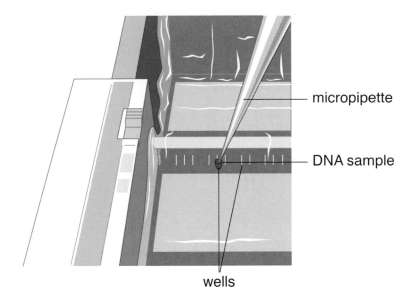

Figure 3

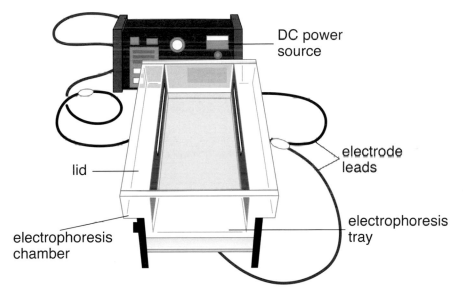

Figure 4

Analysis

1. What is the purpose of gel electrophoresis?
2. During gel electrophoresis, what is the function of the comb?
3. During gel electrophoresis, what is the function of the power supply?

4. Examine Figure 5, which shows bands of DNA in an agarose gel. Which DNA particles move through the agarose gel the fastest, large or small ones?

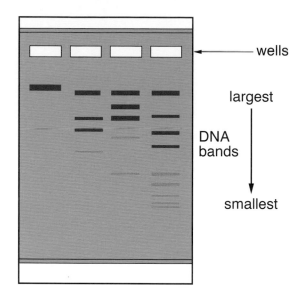

Figure 5

5. Are any two of the DNA fingerprints in Figure 5 exactly alike? Why or why not?

6. Describe the appearance of the gel and the DNA samples after the power supply was removed. Sketch the gel and DNA samples in your science notebook.

7. What is a DNA fingerprint?

8. How do you think that DNA fingerprints can be used to help solve crimes?

9. Would you expect your DNA fingerprint to be exactly like the DNA fingerprint of:

   a. your best friend?

   b. your parents?

   c. your brother or sister?

   d. your identical twin?

   Explain your answers.

10. Create a flow chart or graphic organizer that shows the steps of gel electrophoresis.

What's Going On?

DNA is a macromolecule in the nuclei of cells that carries genetic information. Each strand of DNA is made up of chains of nucleotides, half of which were donated by the mother and the other half by the father. Because of the way cells divide, the likelihood that any two people will inherit the same combination of nucleotides is very slim.

Gel electrophoresis makes it possible to differentiate the DNA of individuals. After a sample of DNA is cut into fragments with restriction enzymes, the fragments are injected into an agarose gel. When the agarose gel is placed in an electrical field, negatively charged pieces of DNA are pulled toward the positive pole in the electrophoresis chamber. Small segments move through the agarose gel faster than large ones. The final arrangement of segments on the gel is unique for each person.

Connections

DNA can be collected at crime scenes and used to identify individuals. DNA is found in all body tissues, and can also be collected from sweat, urine, feces, fingernails, and the roots of hairs. Therefore, good sources of DNA include blood, semen, or swabs from the victim's body. DNA can even be removed from the saliva on the back of a used postage stamp or from a tooth or skeleton. If the DNA fingerprint from a crime scene matches the DNA of a suspect, there is a very good chance that police have their criminal.

 Want to Know More?

See appendix for Our Findings.

Further Reading

Beckmann, Roger. "From Fingerprints to DNA." ABC Materials. Originally published in *Helix*, October/November 2001. Available online. URL: http://www.abc.net.au/science/slab/forensic/default.htm. Accessed April 15, 2008. Produced by ABC, this is a great Web site on Forensic Science.

Brinton, Kate, and Kim-An Lieberman. "Basics of DNA Fingerprinting," May 1994. Available online. URL: http://protist.biology.washington.edu/fingerprint/dnaintro.html. Accessed April 15, 2008. Supported by the University of Washington, this Web site offers basic information on the structure of DNA and the process of DNA fingerprinting.

DNA Learning Center, Cold Springs Harbor Laboratory. "Gene Almanac: Gel Electrophoresis." Available online. URL: http://www.dnalc.org/ddnalc/resources/electrophoresis.html. Accessed April 15, 2008. Created by the Dolan DNA Learning Center, the animation on this Web site shows the steps involved in gel electrophoresis.

7. Probative Value of Class Evidence

Topic

The probability that evidence can be valuable in solving a case can be calculated.

Introduction

Physical evidence can be invaluable in demonstrating that a crime has been committed or to show a link between the crime and victim or between the crime and perpetrator. Physical evidence is classified into two major categories: individual and class. Individual evidence is any type of physical evidence that can be linked to a specific source (so it establishes individuality). Examples of individual evidence include fingerprints and DNA (see Figure 1). Class evidence has characteristics that can only be associated with a group, never a single source. Soil, hair, and manufactured goods are examples of class evidence.

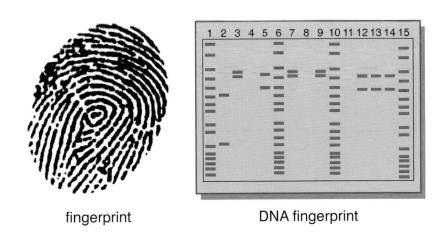

fingerprint   DNA fingerprint

Figure 1

The best kind of evidence for linking a suspect to a crime is individual evidence. A suspect's DNA or fingerprint at a crime scene proves with some certainly that he or she was there. However, class evidence can also help point to an individual. Several pieces of class evidence link a suspect to a scene with greater probability than a single piece. In other words, the more pieces of evidence there are to link a person to a crime, the greater the *probative value* of the evidence. Probative value is the ability of evidence to prove that something is related to a crime.

In a high school, surveillance video cameras captured the image of a person taking laptops from a classroom. The camera showed that the thief had on a black shirt, jeans, and white athletic shoes. Many students may have on one of these items, but it is unlikely that a large number will be wearing all three. The probative value of all three pieces of evidence is relatively high. In this experiment, you will determine the probative value of this person's clothing in your school.

Is this the thief?

Time Required

40 minutes

Materials

- calculator (optional)
- science notebook

Safety Note   Please review and follow the safety guidelines at the beginning of this volume.

Procedure

1. Copy Data Table 1 in your science notebook.

2. Determine the likelihood that a student at your school will be wearing a black shirt. To do so:

   a. Count the number of students in your class and record that number in your science notebook.

   b. Determine the number of students in your class who are wearing a black shirt. Write that number in column A of Data Table 1 in the row labeled "black shirt."

   c. Determine the percentage of students in your class wearing a black shirt. To do so, divide the number of student wearing a black shirt (from column A) by the total number of students in the class.

   For example: if there are 30 students in your class and 10 are wearing a black shirt, your calculations would look like the following:

   $$\text{Percentage in Class} = \frac{10}{30}$$

   $$= 0.33 \text{ (written as a decimal)}$$

   $$= 0.33 \times 100$$

   $$= 33\% \text{ (written as a percentage)}$$

   Record your answer (as a percentage) in column B of Data Table 1.

   c. Determine the probable number of students in your school who are wearing black shirts. To do so, multiply the decimal value of the percentage in column B by the number of students in your school. For example, if there are 1,000 students in your school, your calculations would look like the following:

   Number of students in school wearing black shirt $= 0.33 \times 1,000$

   $$= 330 \text{ students}$$

   Record you answer in column C.

3. Repeat these calculations for students wearing jeans. Record your answers on Data Table 1.

Data Table 1			
	A. Number students in classroom	B. Percentage of students in classroom with this evidence	C. Probable number of students in school with this evidence
Black shirt			
Jeans			
White athletic shoes			

4. Repeat these calculations for students wearing white athletic shoes. Record your answers on Data Table 1.

5. Find the probability that a student in your class is wearing a black shirt, blue jeans, and white athletic shoes. To do so, multiply:
   ✔ percentage (expressed as a decimal) of students wearing a black shirt (column B) by
   ✔ percentage (expressed as a decimal) of students wearing jeans (column B) by
   ✔ percentage (expressed as a decimal) of students wearing white athletic shoes (column B).

   For example, if 33 percent of the students in your class are wearing a black shirt, 50 percent are wearing jeans, and 50 percent are wearing white athletic shoes, you calculations would look like this.

   $$.33 \times .50 \times .50 = 0.0825$$

6. Find out how many students at your school might be dressed in this fashion. To do so, multiply the answer in step 5 by the number of students in school (refer back to the example above). If 1,000 students attend your school, your calculation would look like this:

   $$0.0825 \times 1,000 = 82.5 \text{ (or 82) students}$$

Analysis

1. In an office, 50 individuals have brown hair, 24 have blond hair, 5 have red hair, and 17 have black hair. What percentage of people in the office has blond hair?

2. The office complex employs 212 individuals. How many people in the complex have blond hair?

3. A hit-and-run driver smashed into a parked car and roared away from the scene. Witnesses said that the driver was a female driving a blue Jeep™. To calculate the number of people in your town who fit this description, what information do you need?

4. What is the difference in class evidence and individual evidence?

5. Identify each of the types of physical evidence listed on Data Table 2 as individual evidence or class evidence and explain why.

Data Table 2		
Evidence	**Individual or class?**	**Why?**
a. DNA		
b. Fingerprint		
c. Torn piece of paper		
d. Pair of winter gloves		
e. Handcuffs		

6. Why is it useful to know the probative value of evidence?

7. Why does individual evidence have high probative value?

8. Explain the circumstances in which class evidence can have high probative value.

What's Going On?

Crime scene investigators always hope to find a critical piece of evidence that has individual characteristics. However, this is rarely the case. Most evidence possesses class characteristics and cannot be associated with a single source. Despite this fact, class evidence can help associate an individual with a crime if there is a lot of it. To find the significance of all pieces of class evidence, investigators can apply the *product rule*, a formula to determine probative value, or show how frequently a particular combination of characteristics is found in a population. The product rule states that multiplying the frequency of each piece of evidence will give the probability of finding that evidence in a group.

Connections

Assessing evidence with class characteristics is difficult because so many of the everyday items in our lives are mass produced. If a criminalist locates duct tape and red carpet fibers at a crime scene, he may not have enough evidence to track down the perpetrator. Duct tape is mass produced, so finding a suspect with a roll of duct tape is not very incriminating. Red carpet has multiple sources of production and is common in homes and business. Finding a few red carpet fibers on a suspect is of little value. However, duct tape and red carpet taken together have a high probative value. A suspect with both pieces of evidence would be very suspicious.

As time passes, the value of certain types of class evidence may change. For example, Gremlin was a subcompact car made by American Motor Corporation from 1970 to 1979. The appearance of a Gremlin in the commission of a hit-and-run accident in 1979 was not unusual. At that time, there were about 670,000 Gremlins in the United States. However, the involvement of the same car in a crime in 2008 would be uncommon. Gremlins are fairly rare now, thus the probability that they would be on the road, much less involved in crime, is much lower. This increases the probative value of a Gremlin as physical evidence in a crime.

Want to Know More?

See appendix for Our Findings.

Further Reading

Demumbreum, Rhonda. "Forensic Notes." TeacherWeb, April 22, 2008. Available online. URL: http://teacherweb.com/SC/JFByrnesHS/Demumbreum/faq3.stm#q3. Accessed May 18, 2008. Rhonda Demumbreum of James F. Byrnes High School in Duncan, South Carolina, outlines her entire forensics class lecture.

Forensic Dentistry Online. "Contentious Areas of Human Bitemarks." From an article originally published in *Science and Justice*, April 2001. Available online. URL: http://www.forensicdentistryonline.org/Forensic_pages_1/currentopic1.htm. Accessed May 18, 2008. This Web site discusses how to use the product rule when comparing human bite marks.

Northwest Arkansas Community College. "Physical Evidence, Identification and Comparison." Available online. URL: http://www.nwacc.edu/academics/criminaljustice/documents/PhysicalEvidence.pdf. Accessed May 18, 2008. Presented as an outline, this Web site provides an excellent lesson on physical evidence and probative value.

8. Blood Spatter Inquiry

Topic

The shapes of bloodstains are affected by the textures of surfaces on which they fall.

Introduction

When a droplet of blood comes in contact with a surface, it may or may not spatter. However, it will form a bloodstain. Figure 1 shows how a droplet of blood behaves when it hits a surface. A falling droplet is almost spherical in shape. When the droplet hits a surface, the lower edge of the droplet is deformed and blood is forced outward to form a border. At a crime scene, patterns made by the borders of blood droplets are clues that help solve the crime.

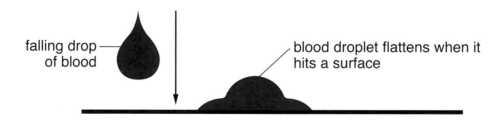

falling drop of blood

blood droplet flattens when it hits a surface

Figure 1

After a crime has been discovered, a crime scene investigation (CSI) technician determines the location, distribution, and appearance of bloodstains. As she works, a CSI tech photographs, measures, and describes the blood evidence. All the information gathered by the technician is turned over to bloodstain pattern experts for interpretation.

To be an expert in bloodstain pattern interpretation, one must study the behavior of blood under a variety of circumstances. Tests must be conducted to find out how temperature, height, force of impact, and other factors affect the shapes and arrangements of bloodstains. By working with blood and studying the patterns that blood makes in different situations, experts can use bloodstains to help them reconstruct the events of a crime. In this experiment, you will take on the role of a bloodstain pattern expert who wants to know how the texture of a target's surface affects the pattern of blood spatter.

Time Required

55 minutes

Materials

- artificial blood
- droppers or pipettes
- metersticks
- rulers
- smooth tile (one square)
- textured linoleum (one square)
- small mirror
- small square of aluminum foil
- paper towels
- science notebook

Safety Note   Please review and follow the safety guidelines at the beginning of this volume.

Procedure

1. Your job is to design and perform an experiment to find out how the textures of three different surfaces affect the size and shape of bloodstains.

2. You can use any of the supplies provided by your teacher, but you will not need to use all of them. If you would like to use additional supplies, consult with your teacher to see if they are available.

3. Before you conduct your experiment, decide exactly what you are

going to do. Write the steps you plan to take (your experimental procedure) and the materials you plan to use (materials list) on the data table. Show your procedure and materials list to the teacher. If you get teacher approval, proceed with your experiment. If not, modify your work and show it to your teacher again.

4. As you design your experiment, keep these points in mind:

   a. Control all variables except the one you are testing: texture of the target surface (the surface onto which the blood falls). Variables include, but are not limited to, the amount of blood in each droplet, the height from which blood is dropped, and the angle at which blood strikes a surface.

   b. Carry out several trials in your experiment. For example, drop blood 10 times from a prescribed height onto one type of surface. Then drop blood 10 times from the same height onto a different surface.

   c. Keep accurate records as you do your experiment. Records can include descriptions, measurements, and drawings.

5. Once you have teacher approval, assemble the materials you need and begin your procedure.

6. Collect your results on a data table of your own design.

Analysis

1. How does blood spatter analysis help solve crimes?

2. Why does an investigator need to know the texture of the target surface?

3. During this experiment, you had to control for several variables. Name those variables.

4. What conclusions did you draw from your experiments?

5. Suggest a follow-up experiment that would be a logical next step of your experiment.

6. Examine the blood drops A and B in Figure 2 on page 52. One fell on a smooth, untextured floor surface. The other fell on a porous plastic tile. Which droplet fell on the porous tile? Explain your answer.

Data Table	
Your experimental procedure	
Your materials list	
Teacher's approval	

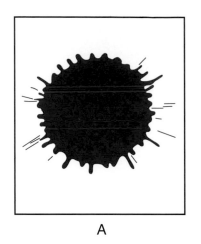
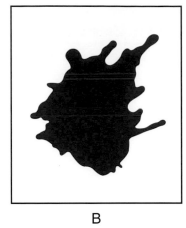

A

B

Figure 2

What's Going On?

When a drop of blood hits a target surface, it forms a stain with or without spattering. The size of the bloodstain is determined by the amount of blood. The overall shape of the stain depends on the angle at which a blood drop hits a surface as well as the speed at which the blood drop was traveling. More subtle characteristics of the shape of a bloodstain are due to the texture of the target surface.

Glass and metal are very hard smooth surfaces that most often yield rounded stains. This pattern is due to the fact that smooth materials offer less surface area to deflect the liquid. Highly textured material, like linoleum, cardboard, or newspaper, produces stains with jagged edges. Blood drops falling on a textured target may show scalloping or spines extending from the droplet.

Connections

Blood is primarily composed of water. By understanding water, an expert can better understand the behavior of blood. Like water, blood displays *surface tension* because individual particles within a drop are attracted to each other. This *cohesive* property of blood tends to hold droplets together.

Although blood spatter evidence can be useful to investigators, it is not always available. Some surfaces, like fabrics, absorb blood and destroy the pattern of droplets. Many outdoor surfaces are water resistant, so blood does not stick. If a bloodstain becomes smudged or smeared, it cannot be interpreted. Such a loss of valuable evidence can slow the interpretation of a crime scene.

Want to Know More?

See appendix for Our Findings.

Further Reading

Akin, Lois L. "Blood Spatter, Interpretation at Crime Scenes." Bloodspatter. Originally published in *The Forensic Examiner*, Summer 2005. Available online. URL: http://www.bloodspatter.com/bloodspatter. pdf. Accessed May 1, 2008. Pictures and well-written text make this Web site a fascinating resource on blood spatter evidence.

Centre for Learning Technology, University of Western Australia. "Forensic Investigations: Blood Spatter, Properties of Blood." Available online. URL: http://www.clt.uwa.edu.au/__data/page/112508/fsb05.pdf. Accessed May 18, 2008. These Web pages are part of a program designed to help students learn how analytical and critical thinking can help solve questions related to forensics.

Slemko, Joseph A. "Bloodstains on Fabric, The Effects of Droplet Velocity and Fabric Composition," International Association of Bloodstain Pattern Analysts. Available online. URL: http://www.iabpa.org/ December2003News.pdf. Accessed May 1, 2008. An interesting follow-up experiment to this laboratory would be to determine how various fabrics affect blood spatter. This article provides some fascinating insights.

9. Specific Gravity of Body Fluids

Topic

Specific gravity is a measurement that is useful in forensic science.

Introduction

All matter has two basic characteristics: *mass* and *volume*. In the laboratory, the mass of a sample can be determined with an electronic scale or triple-beam balance. Typically, mass is measured in units such as ounces (oz) or grams (g). The amount of space that an object occupies, its volume, can be found in two ways: a regularly shaped solid is measured with a ruler or tape measure, as shown in Figure 1, in units such as square inches or cubic centimeters. The volume of a liquid can easily be found in a graduated cylinder and measured in milliliters (ml).

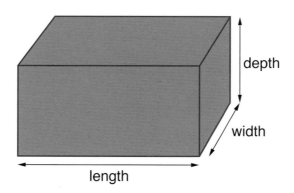

Figure 1

Once the mass and volume of a substance are known, a third quantity can be calculated: *density*. To find the density of a sample of matter, the mass of that matter is divided by its volume. The formula for determining density is:

$$D = \frac{m}{v}$$

where *D* is density, *m* is mass, and *v* is volume.

One way to analyze the meaning of a material's density is by comparing it to the density of water. *Specific gravity* is the ratio of the density of a substance to the density of water. This relationship can be stated as a formula:

$$SG = \frac{D_1}{D_w}$$

where SG represents specific gravity, D_1 is the density of a material and D_w is the density of equal volume of water. In this experiment, you will learn how to find the specific gravity of a liquid.

Time Required

55 minutes

Materials

- 20 ml of blood sample 1
- 20 ml of blood sample 2
- 20 ml of urine sample 1
- 20 ml of urine sample 2
- electronic scale
- 100-ml graduated cylinder
- access to water
- science notebook

Safety Note Please review and follow the safety guidelines at the beginning of this volume.

Procedure

1. Find the density of water. To do so:
   a. Determine the mass of a dry, 100-ml graduated cylinder. Record the mass on Data Table 1.
   b. Add 10 ml of water to the graduated cylinder. Determine the mass of the graduated cylinder and water. Subtract the mass of the graduated cylinder. Record the mass of water on Data Table 1.

c. Determine the density of the water sample. To do so, divide the mass of the water by its volume. Record the density on Data Table 1.

d. Add another 10 ml of water to the graduated cylinder. Determine the mass of the water. Record the mass of the water on Data Table 1.

e. Determine the density of the water sample and record it on Data Table 1.

f. Repeat steps d and e until you have 100 ml of water in the graduated cylinder.

g. Find the average density of your calculations. To do so, add the densities of all 10 water samples and divide by 10. Record the average density on the last row of Data Table 1.

Data Table 1		
	Mass (grams) [g]	**Density (g/ml)**
Empty graduated cylinder		NA
10 ml water		
20 ml water		
30 ml water		
40 ml water		
50 ml water		
60 ml water		
70 ml water		
80 ml water		
90 ml water		
100 ml water		
Average	NA	

2. Repeat step 1 to find the density of each of the samples provided by your teacher. Create four more Data Tables in your science notebook like Data Table 1. Title these data tables as "Blood Sample 1," "Blood Sample 2," "Urine Sample 1," and "Urine Sample 2."

3. Once you have the density of each sample, calculate the specific gravity of each sample. Refer to the Introduction to review the formula for specific gravity. Record the specific gravity for each sample on Data Table 2.

Data Table 2	
Material	**Specific gravity**
Sample 1	
Sample 2	
Sample 3	
Sample 4	

Analysis

1. Define "density."
2. Did the density of water vary depending on the volume of water?
3. The accepted density of water is 1 g/ml. Determine the accuracy of your calculation (of average density) by finding your percent error. To do so, use the formula:

$$\text{Percent error} = \frac{(\text{your calculation} - \text{accepted density})}{\text{accepted density})} \times 100$$

4. Define "specific gravity."
5. Consider your findings for samples 1 and 2. Both are blood samples. Of the two, which was more likely removed from the heart of a drowning victim? (*Hint:* in a drowning victim, blood in the heart may be diluted by water.) Explain your answer.
6. Consider your findings for samples 3 and 4, the urine samples. Which one more likely contains additional proteins and minerals? Explain your answer.

What's Going On?

Specific gravity is a measurement that is used in labs to compare the density of a sample to the density of water. Like density, specific gravity is independent of the size of the sample. Specific gravity is described as "dimensionless" because it is simply a ratio and is not expressed in units. Materials whose specific gravity is less than 1 will float on water; those with specific gravity greater than 1 sink in water.

Several types of instruments can measure specific gravity. One is the *hydrometer*, a glass cylinder topped with a rubber bulb. The cylinder contains a float. If the liquid you are testing has a specific gravity greater than water, the float will rise in the column of liquid. The float sinks in the column of liquid if its specific gravity is lower than water.

Connections

Specific gravity is a measurement that is useful in many types of forensic cases. In some situations, accurate urine testing is useful in solving a case. However, urine samples may be purposefully corrupted to hide drug use. A low specific gravity indicates urine dilution caused by drinking large quantities of water. If a person is asked to take a urine drug test, a dramatic dilution suggests that the person is trying to alter the test results by flushing chemicals from his body. The normal range of specific gravity in urine varies from 1.003 to 1.030. Tests that reveal values outside of this range suggest specimen dilution or alteration.

Pathologists may also need to use specific gravity when drowning is the suspected cause of death. Inhalation of water dramatically alters blood chemistry. When water enters the lungs, it is immediately absorbed into the blood, diluting it. As this diluted blood leaves the lungs, it travels through the pulmonary vein into the left atrium of the heart. From this chamber, the diluted blood enters the left ventricle (see Figure 2). The heart cannot pump diluted blood and it stops functioning. The specific gravity of diluted blood is lower than normal blood. Therefore, a difference in specific gravity between the left and right ventricles may indicate to a pathologist that drowning is the cause of death.

Want to Know More?

See appendix for Our Findings.

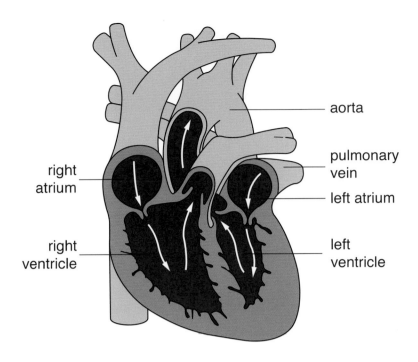

Figure 2

The human heart

Further Reading

Medline Plus. "Urine Specific Gravity," Medlineplus. Available online. URL: http://www.nlm.nih.gov/medlineplus/ency/article/003587.htm. Accessed May 21, 2008. Updated on September 22, 2007. This Web site, supported by the U.S. National Library of Medicine and the National Institutes of Health, provides accurate information on the procedures involved in checking the specific gravity of urine.

Safety Emporium. "Density, Specific Gravity," MSDS HyperGlossary. Available online. URL: http://www.ilpi.com/msds/ref/density.html. Accessed May 21, 2008. Updated on May 18, 2006. Supported by Safety Emporium, this Web site shows a glass hydrometer and explains how to use it.

United States Environmental Protection Agency. "Module 4: Liquid Characteristics—Density and Specific Gravity," Available online. URL: http://www.epa.gov/apti/bces/module4/gravity/gravity.htm. Accessed May 21, 2008. Updated April 4, 2008. This online lesson offered by the EPA offers students to opportunity to better understand and work with the concepts of density and specific gravity.

10. Soil Identification

Topic

Soil is a type of physical evidence that can be identified by its characteristics.

Introduction

Soil can be a key player in solving some investigations. In forensics, soil is considered to be the broken down material on the Earth's surface. Soil may contain decayed plant and animal matter, minerals and rocks, as well as a variety of tiny pieces of man-made materials like paint, plastic, and glass. The presence of these types of manufactured material makes soil unique to an area, and can be helpful in identifying its source.

Soil that is lacking artificial debris is harder to tie to a specific region. Even so, the natural characteristics of soil can sometimes be used to trace soil to a region. One of the naturally occurring traits of soil that are usually assessed in an investigation is particle size. In this experiment, you will examine the particle size of a sample of soil from a crime scene and three samples of local soils to see if you can find a match.

Time Required

10 minutes on day 1
55 minutes on day 2

Materials

- ❖ 4 aluminum pie plates
- ❖ soil sample from "crime scene"
- ❖ soil sample A
- ❖ soil sample B
- ❖ soil sample C

- soil sieve (mesh #10, retains gravel)
- soil sieve (mesh #230, retains sand)
- soil sieve (mesh 5 microns, retains silt)
- measuring cup or 400-milliliter (ml) beaker
- triple-beam balance or electronic scale
- paper towels
- sheet of newspaper
- masking tape or labels
- science notebook

Safety Note   Please review and follow the safety guidelines at the beginning of this volume.

Procedure, Day 1

1. Label the four pie plates Crime Scene, A, B, and C. Spread about one-half cup (or about 200 ml) of each soil sample in the appropriate pie plate. Set the pie plates aside to dry overnight.

Procedure, Day 2

1. Weigh a paper towel and record its weight in your science notebook.

2. Pour 200 ml of soil from the "crime scene" onto the paper towel and find their combined weight. Subtract the weight of the paper towel from the weight of the soil and paper towel to find the weight of the soil. Record the soil's weight (in grams [g]) in the appropriate row of the data table in the column titled "Crime Scene."

3. Spread a sheet of newspaper on the floor. Examine the soil sieves and select the one that retains gravel (see Figure 1). This will be the sieve with the largest holes. Pour the crime scene soil sample into the sieve while holding the sieve over the newspaper. Gently shake the sieve until there is no more soil passing through. (You may want to cover the top of the sieve with a sheet of notebook paper to reduce dust.) The soil left in the sieve is the gravel fraction of your sample. Pour the gravel fraction onto a paper towel and find its weight. (Remember to subtract the weight of the paper towel.)

Record the weight of the gravel fraction in the second row of the data table in the column labeled "Crime Scene." Set the gravel aside.

Figure 1

Soil sieves

4. Collect the soil that fell onto the newspaper. Spread another piece of newspaper on the floor. Pour the soil into the sand sieve while holding the sieve over the newspaper. Gently shake the sieve until there is no more soil passing through. (You may want to cover the top of the sieve with a sheet of notebook paper to reduce dust.) The soil left in the sieve is the sand fraction of your sample. Pour the sand fraction onto a paper towel and find its weight. (Remember to subtract the weight of the paper towel.) Record the weight of the sand fraction in the second row of the data table in the column labeled "Crime Scene." Set the sand aside.

5. Collect the soil that fell onto the newspaper. Spread another piece of newspaper on the floor. Pour the soil into the silt sieve while holding the sieve over the newspaper. Gently shake the sieve until there is no more soil passing through. (You may want to cover the top of the sieve with a sheet of notebook paper to reduce dust.) The soil left in the sieve is the silt fraction of your sample. Pour the silt fraction onto a paper towel and find its weight. (Remember to subtract the weight of the paper towel.) Record the weight of the silt fraction in the second row of the data table in the column labeled "Crime Scene." Set the silt aside.

6. The material that passed through the silt sieve is the clay fraction. Place the clay fraction onto a paper towel, find its weight, and record the weight on the data table in the row labeled "Clay fraction."

7. Calculate the percentage of each soil fraction of the crime scene sample using the following formulas. Record your calculations in your science notebook.

   a. (Weight of gravel) ÷ (Weight of entire sample) x 100
      = _____ % gravel

   b. (Weight of sand) ÷ (Weight of entire sample) x 100
      = _____ % sand

   c. (Weight of silt) ÷ (Weight of entire sample) x 100
      = _____ % silt

   d. (Weight of clay) ÷ (Weight of entire sample) x 100
      = _____ % clay

8. Add the four percentages to see if they equal about 100 percent. If so, your calculations are most likely correct. If not, check your calculations.

9. Repeat steps 2 through 8 for soil samples A, B, and C. Record all data in the appropriate parts of the data table.

Data Table				
	Weight			
	Crime Scene	**A**	**B**	**C**
Soil sample				
Gravel fraction				
Sand fraction				
Silt fraction				
Clay fraction				

Analysis

1. Which soil sample (A, B, or C) was most like the crime scene sample?

2. In this experiment, you examined particle size of soil. Name two other characteristics of soil that may be useful in identifying a sample.

3. How did the three sieves differ?

4. How might soil analysis help show whether the victim of a homicide had been moved from the scene of the shooting?

5. On the tires of a car involved in a crime, an investigator found soil that contains fragments of bricks. How might this soil help the investigator?

6. An expert on physical evidence examined a soil sample from a crime scene. The entire sample weighed 100 g. By sieving, he concluded that 2 g were gravel, 33 g were sand, 30 g were silt, and 34 g were clay. Next the expert referred to his records and found that soil in the mountainous part of his state is 20 percent sand, soil in the coastal plain is 30 to 50 percent sand, and soil along the coast is 80 percent sand.

   a. What percentage of the soil sample is sand?

   b. From what region of the state was this sample most likely taken?

   c. What other information might help this expert locate the source of the sample?

What's Going On?

Soil is one type of physical evidence that can help link a suspect's shoes, clothing, or car to a crime scene. In the crime scene laboratory, soil is examined in several ways. Low-powered microscopic analysis can identify the characteristics of particles that make up the soil. Knowledge of minerals and rocks can enable the expert to characterize the soil and possibly determine its point of origin.

Physical characteristics of soil are valuable in making comparisons. Color is always considered when comparing soil samples. Since all soils are darker when wet, samples are dried before their colors are judged. Scientists have identified more than 1,000 different colors in soil.

Lab analysis can include a density-gradient tube, which reveals the density distribution of soil. Inside a thin glass tube, liquids of several different densities are layered. When soil is added to the tube, its particles sink to the level where density is equal to its own.

Because soil is ubiquitous and easily transferred from one location to another, techniques for characterizing it are still being developed. Reference specimens from regions are routinely collected and analyzed for future use. Since only the uppermost layer is usually picked up during the commission of a crime, specimens are taken from the topmost layers.

Connections

The case of the disappearance of Alice Redmond was solved by Georgia police with the help of soil identification. Alice's friend, Mark Miller, stated that he picked up Alice after work and the two of them drove around for a while before he took her home. Police were suspicious of the boyfriend's story, but had no evidence to disprove it.

Within a short time, Alice's missing car was located in the parking lot of the local hospital. Police interviewed Mark again and looked at his car. Mud was thick over the car's wheel wells and undercarriage (see Figure 2). Close inspection showed that the mud was actually made up of two distinct layers. The underlayer was reddish brown, like the local soil. The thick, upper layer was deep brown, unlike anything in the vicinity. However, the brown soil was typical of a region in Alabama near a garbage dump. Officers searched the dump and found Alice's body. Soil samples from the tires and from the dump were dried and their colors were compared. The two soils were then sieved and their particle sizes compared. The soil on Mark's tires and soil at the dump where the body were found were found to be consistent. This strong soil evidence helped prosecute Mark for the murder of his girlfriend.

Figure 2
An officer examines the car tires.

Want to Know More?

See appendix for Our Findings.

Further Reading

Center for Australian Forensic Science. "How Soil Evidence Helped Solve a Double Murder Case." Commonwealth Scientific and Industrial Research Organisation. Available online. URL: http://www.csiro.au/files/files/p9ng.pdf. Accessed May 17, 2008. Excellent pictures make this an interesting site for learning more about soil as evidence.

Interpol. "Forensic Examination of Soil Evidence." 13th Interpol Forensic Science Symposium. Available online. URL: http://www.interpol.int/Public/Forensic/IFSS/meeting13/Reviews/Soil.pdf. Accessed May 17, 2008. Written by Interpol, this article provides detailed information on how soil can be used to help solve crimes, and it gives some interesting examples.

Spector, Christy. "Secrets Hidden in Soil." Soil Science Education. Available online. URL: http://soil.gsfc.nasa.gov/forengeo/secret.htm. Accessed May 17, 2008. This Web site, hosted by NASA, offers an excellent summary of soil characteristics and the types of analyses that can be done by forensic investigators and other scientists. This selection is based on work by geologists R. Murray and J. Tedrow.

11. Density of Glass

Topic

The density of glass can be found using fluids of known densities.

Introduction

Glass, an important part of everyday life, is also used to make items used routinely in the science laboratory—everything from beakers to the lens in microscopes. Glass is produced by melting a silica compound and shaping the amorphous product into the desired form. When cooled, the shape holds and the object becomes brittle and solid. Additional compounds, such as lead, are often added to the silica in order to produce desired qualities such as color or extra sparkle.

Additives affect the *density* of glass. Different types of glass have different chemicals in them, causing varying densities. For example, glass made with lead—a very dense element—is denser than glass made with boron, a less-dense element. In many cases the density of glass, or properties affected by the density, can help determine the source of broken glass found at a crime scene. The principle of buoyancy can be used to determine the density of a piece of glass.

Items are *buoyant*, or able to float, only when they are less dense than the liquid in which they are floating. When a piece of glass is the same density as the liquid in which it is submerged, then it will neither float to the top of the liquid nor sink to the bottom. Instead the glass will remain suspended within the solution. In this experiment, you will use a solution of sugar water to calculate the density of three different pieces of glass.

Time Required

35 minutes

Materials

- ➣ 100-milliliters (ml) graduated cylinder
- ➣ 150-ml beaker
- ➣ 3 small pieces of glass of varying densities
- ➣ 225 ml distilled water
- ➣ stirring rod
- ➣ pair of tongs
- ➣ 250 grams (g) sugar
- ➣ electronic balance
- ➣ science notebook

Safety Note   Take care when working with glass. Please review and follow the safety guidelines at the beginning of this volume.

Procedure

1. Use the electronic balance to find the mass of the empty, dry beaker. Record this value on the data table.

2. Add approximately 75 ml of distilled water to the beaker.

3. Place the first piece of glass into the beaker of water. Use the stirring rod to make sure that the piece of glass is completely submerged.

4. Slowly add sugar to the water, stirring carefully after each addition to ensure that the piece of glass lifts off the bottom of the beaker each time. Add sugar until the piece of glass is suspended in the solution.

5. Carefully remove the piece of glass with the tongs.

6. Use the electronic balance to find the mass of the solution and the beaker. Subtract the mass of the beaker to find the mass of just the sugar solution. Record this mass on the data table.

7. Carefully pour the sugar solution into the graduated cylinder. Record the volume of the sugar solution on the data table.

8. Clean and dry the beaker.

9. Assuming that the density of the glass is the same as the density of the sugar solution in which it was suspended, use the equation $D = m/V$ to calculate the density of the glass. In this equation, D represents density, m stands for mass, and V is volume. Record the density of the glass on the data table.

10. Repeat steps 2 through 9 for the second and third pieces of glass.

Data Table				
	Mass of beaker (g)	**Mass of sugar solution (g)**	**Volume of sugar solution (ml)**	**Density of glass (g/ml)**
Sample 1				
Sample 2				
Sample 3				

Analysis

1. Why did the addition of sugar to the water change the density of the water?

2. Which glass sample was the densest? Could you tell this just by looking at the glass?

3. What kinds of uses do you think might require low-density glass?

4. What kinds of uses do you think might require high-density glass?

5. Does the size of the piece of glass have an effect on its density? Explain your answer.

6. From a forensics standpoint, why would it be important to be able to identify the density of different pieces of glass?

What's Going On?

In this experiment you used a sugar solution to calculate the density of glass samples. The sugar was helpful because you could use it to create a solution of any density. As you added sugar, the density of the water increased due to the higher density of the sugar dissolved inside the water molecules. By creating a solution that was the same density of the piece of the glass, you caused the glass to become suspended in the sugar solution.

Samples of glass vary in density because they differ in composition. The heavier pieces of glass are often made using a lead additive. This type of glass tends to sparkle and is used for crystal (see Figure 1a). The lighter pieces of glass often contain boron. This additive makes the glass more durable and lightweight. Flasks and beakers used in labs are typically made with boron additives (see Figure 1b).

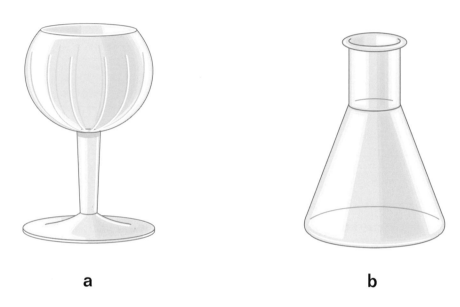

a   b

Figure 1

Connections

Finding the density of a piece of glass is very important to forensic scientists when studying break-ins. For example, if glass found on a suspect can be determined to be the same as glass from a broken window, it links the suspect to the crime scene. Density analysis can also be useful in reconstructing car accidents. Bits of glass can be tested to help determine the relative positions of two cars when their windows broke. More detailed examinations of glass can be used to find its source. Such examinations are based on the fact that type and location of production affects the chemical makeup of the glass. Some common techniques are to analyze the chemical makeup specifically or to calculate the index of refraction of the glass. Window glass commonly has a density ranging from 2.4 g/ml to 2.8 g/ml, while glass from car headlights is about 1.3 to 1.5 g/ml.

Want to Know More?

See appendix for Our Findings.

Further Reading

Forensic Access. "Glass Analysis," *Forensic Access*, 2004. Available online. URL: http://www.forensic-access.co.uk/forensic-access-publications/benchmark-newsletter/glass-analysis.htm. Accessed April 28, 2008. This Web site describes techniques used to determine the source of broken glass and how glass can be used as forensic evidence.

Forensic Science Communications. "Glass Density Determination," *Forensic Science Communications*, Volume 7, Number 1, January 2005. Available online. URL: http://www.fbi.gov/hq/lab/fsc/backissu/jan2005/standards/2005standards8.htm. Accessed April 28, 2008. Several methods for determining the density of glass are described on this Web site.

Gilman, Victoria. "Glass." *Science and Technology*, Volume 81, Number 47, November 24, 2003. Available online. URL: http://pubs.acs.org/cen/whatstuff/stuff/8147glass.html. Accessed May 23, 2008. Gilman explains the basics of the chemistry of glass.

12. Emission Spectra Can Identify Elements

Topic

The emission spectra of unknown chemicals can be used as a form of identification.

Introduction

The identification of unknown chemicals can be crucial in some forensic investigations. One easy way to identify an unknown liquid is through its *emission spectrum*, the wavelength of light given off by a chemical when it burns or otherwise absorbs energy. Every chemical releases a unique color of light during combustion. If that color is viewed with an electroscope or prism, it is broken down into bands of individual colors in a manner that is similar to the separation of white light into the colors of the rainbow (see Figure 1).

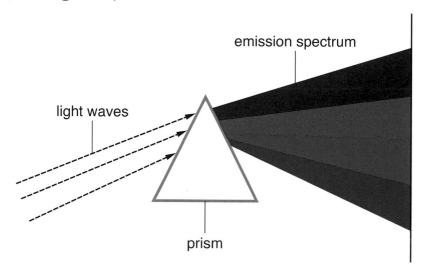

Figure 1

The individual bands of color revealed by an electroscope are unique to a specific element. For example, hydrogen gas emits a pinkish color when burned or when electricity passes through it. When that color is viewed with an electroscope or a prism, distinct bands of color appear: a red band, a yellowish-green band, and several shades of blue (see Figure 2).

Figure 2

Hydrogen emission spectrum

The emission spectrum is unique for each element, so it can be used to identify that chemical just as a fingerprint can be used to identify an individual. While not every chemical releases light that is in the visible spectrum, many compounds, particularly the alkaline metals, produce bright colors. Many laboratories identify elements with machines that automatically burn the chemical, read the emission spectrum, and match it up to a list of known chemicals. This technique is most commonly employed to identify the metals in a compound. In this experiment you will identify unknown chemicals using their emission spectra.

Time Required

40 minutes

Materials

- ✦ hot plate
- ✦ Bunsen burner
- ✦ striker
- ✦ wooden splints
- ✦ 250-milliliter (ml) Erlenmeyer flask
- ✦ tongs
- ✦ spot plate
- ✦ cotton swabs
- ✦ 5 unknown alkaline solutions
- ✦ access to chemistry textbook or chemistry resource book
- ✦ science notebook

Safety Note   Wear goggles and gloves when working with chemicals. Take special care when working with the hot plate. Please review and follow the safety guidelines at the beginning of this volume.

Procedure

1. Your job is to design and perform an experiment to determine the identity of the unknown chemicals using the colors they produce in a flame.

2. You can use any of the supplies provided by your teacher, but you will not need to use all of them.

3. Before you conduct your experiment, decide exactly what you are going to do. Write the steps you plan to take (your experimental procedure) and the materials you plan to use (materials list) on the data table below. Show your procedure and materials list to the teacher. If you get teacher approval, proceed with your experiment. If not, modify your work and show it to your teacher again.

4. Once you have teacher approval, assemble the materials you need and begin your procedure.

5. Collect your results on a data table of your own design.

Analysis

1. What was the identity of each of the unknown chemicals?

    Unknown 1 _____   Unknown 4 _____

    Unknown 2 _____   Unknown 5 _____

    Unknown 3 _____

2. What did you use as your source of energy?

3. Why was a source of energy necessary?

4. What is one source of error for your experiment?

5. If you did this experiment again, what would you do differently?

What's Going On?

In this experiment, energy is added to a chemical in the form of heat. When the chemical absorbs energy, electrons within its atoms become "excited." Electrons are arranged on energy levels that surround the nucleus of the atom. These levels can be thought of as concentric layers, like the layers of an onion. When the electrons become excited, they gain energy and jump to a higher energy level, further away from the nucleus. However, this excited state is unstable and the electrons quickly drop back to their original position, called the ground state. As they drop back, energy that was absorbed by the electrons is released in the form of light. Since all elements have a unique number and arrangement of electrons, the amount of energy released by each element is different. In terms of light, different amounts of energy produce different wavelengths and different colors of light. Some elements even release light in the infrared and ultraviolet range of the spectrum. While we cannot see this light with our naked eyes, electroscopic equipment can detect this type of light.

Data Table	
Your experimental procedure	
Your materials list	
Teacher's approval	

Connections

Atomic emission spectra have dozens of practical applications. In forensics applications, they are used to identify trace evidence left at crime scenes. Unlike many other tests, emission spectrum analysis can be done on very small samples. Emission spectra have many other practical applications. The singular colors given off by neon lights are due to their unique emission spectra. Neon lights work by passing electrical energy through a gas, exciting its electrons and causing the gas to emit a distinct, colored light. Different gases produce different colored neon lights. Astronomers use emission spectra to identify the composition of stars. Since physical samples cannot be taken of distant stars, using the colors of the stars allows scientists to identify their composition. The Environmental Protection Agency (EPA) analyzes emission spectra to identify metal contamination in the environment. This relatively simple chemical analysis provides us with a variety of uses and applications.

Want to Know More?

See appendix for Our Findings.

Further Reading

Exline, David L., Rebecca L. Schuler, and Patrick J. Treado. "Improved Fingerprint Visualization," *Forensic Science Communications*, Volume 5, Number 3, July 2003. Available online. URL: http://www.fbi.gov/hq/lab/fsc/backissu/july2003/exline.htm. Accessed August 27, 2008. This Web page includes a paper that discusses using emission spectra to improve current methods of fingerprint detection and identification.

Forensic Science and Forensic Medicine. "Forensics Microanalysis." Available online. URL: http://www.forensic-medecine.info/forensic-microanalysis.html. Accessed April 28, 2008. This Web site accurately discusses the field of forensics microanalysis, which includes using emission spectra to identify unknown elements.

University of Oregon Physics Department. "Elemental Absorption and Emission Spectra." Available online. URL: http://jersey.uoregon.edu/vlab/elements/Elements.html. Accessed May 19, 2008. This page contains a periodic table with clickable elements. As you click on the element, its absorption or emission spectrum is shown.

13. Comparing Latent Fingerprint Techniques

Topics

Superglue fuming and iodine fuming are two techniques used to preserve latent fingerprints.

Introduction

At a crime scene, investigators seek out any clues that can help them identify the perpetrator. One of the most important types of clues is fingerprints. Some fingerprints are immediately visible, but others are not. The invisible prints are described as *latent*. Materials that may harbor latent prints are often collected and taken back to the forensics laboratory for chemical analysis.

Two effective techniques in chemical analysis of latent prints are superglue fuming and iodine fuming. In both techniques, materials that may have prints are enclosed in a chamber and exposed to chemical fumes. During fuming, a chemical reaction occurs between the fumes and the molecules that make up the fingerprints. This reaction makes the fingerprints visible. Figure 1 shows a chamber ready for superglue fuming.

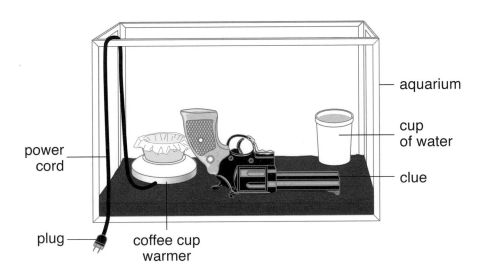

Figure 1

In this experiment, you will use a small, covered aquarium as a fuming chamber for visualizing fingerprints. Within the chamber, you will develop fingerprints on several types of materials first using iodine fumes and then using superglue fumes. You will compare the results of both techniques to see which produce the best prints on each type of material.

Time Required

55 minutes

Materials

- 2 small pieces (about 2 inches [in.] by 2 in. [5 centimeters (cm) by 5 cm]) of tile
- 2 small pieces (about 2 in. by 2 in. [5 cm by 5 cm]) of glass
- 2 small pieces (about 2 in. by 2 in. [5 cm by 5 cm]) of plastic
- 2 small pieces (about 2 in. by 2 in. [5 cm by 5 cm]) of paper
- 2 small pieces (about 2 in. by 2 in. [5 cm by 5 cm]) of wood
- superglue
- iodine crystals (about 2 dozen)
- small aquarium
- cover for aquarium
- aluminum foil
- empty soda can
- coffee cup warmer (or small hot plate)
- small beaker or cup
- hand lens
- access to water
- science notebook

| Safety Note | Wear goggles and gloves while working with chemicals. Work only in a well-ventilated area. Take care when working with the coffee cup warmer. Please review and follow the safety guidelines at the beginning of this volume. |

Procedure: Part A

1. Before you put on your gloves, touch the pieces of tile, glass, plastic, paper, and wood to create fingerprints on all of the surfaces. Try to put the same number of prints on each material. Once prints are made, you can put on your gloves.

2. Place 1 piece of tile, glass, plastic, paper, and wood in the bottom of the aquarium. Arrange the pieces so that they do not touch.

3. Sprinkle several iodine crystals onto a small piece of aluminum foil. Place the crystals in the aquarium near the materials with latent prints.

4. Cover the aquarium and wait 15 minutes.

5. After 15 minutes, remove the materials and examine them for visible prints.

6. Remove the iodine crystals from the aquarium and store them according to your teacher's instructions.

Procedure: Part B

1. Gather the unused pieces of tile, glass, plastic, paper, and wood. Place them in the bottom of the aquarium, arranging them so that they do not touch.

2. Place the coffee cup warmer in the aquarium. Run the power cord over the edge of the aquarium so that it can be plugged in.

3. Make a small bowl, about the size of the palm of your hand, from aluminum foil. Place the aluminum foil bowl on the coffee cup warmer.

4. Place some superglue (about the size of a dime) in the aluminum foil bowl.

5. Place a small beaker or cup of water in the aquarium.

6. Position the cover on the aquarium.

7. Plug up the coffee cup warmer and let it heat the superglue for about 10 minutes.

8. After 10 minutes, turn off the coffee cup warmer and carefully remove the tile, glass, plastic paper, and wood. Examine each item for visible print.

Analysis

1. Look over the materials that were fumed with iodine crystals. Describe the color, shape, and clarity of any fingerprints you see. Use the hand lens if necessary.

2. Look over the materials that were fumed with superglue. Describe the color, shape, and clarity of any fingerprints you see. Use the hand lens if necessary.

3. Complete the data table by putting a check mark in the correct column to show which technique, iodine fuming or superglue fuming, produced the best prints on each type of material.

Data Table		
Material	**Iodine fuming**	**Superglue fuming**
Tile		
Glass		
Plastic		
Paper		
Wood		

4. Reexamine the fingerprints created by both techniques about 15 minutes after fuming. Have any of the fingerprints faded or disappeared? If so, which ones?

5. You are a forensic scientist who has been asked to assess the usefulness of iodine fuming and superglue fuming on tile, glass, plastic, paper, and wood. Write a short letter that explains how to get the best prints on each of these materials.

What's Going On?

Superglue fuming is generally preferred for nonporous substances like metal, glass, and plastic. Superglue contains cyanoacrylate, a strong adhesive. Materials containing latent prints are put in closed chambers in which heat is used to vaporize the liquid glue. Fumes from the warmed cyanoacrylate chemically bond to the oils in fingerprints to produce a white-colored, visible print.

Iodine fuming provides good results on both porous and nonporous surfaces. Materials containing latent prints are put in a closed container with solid iodine. As the iodine *sublimes*, iodine vapors are produced. These combine with the oil and sweat that make up latent prints to yield brownish-red prints that should be photographed immediately. Eventually, the iodine in the print will sublime, leaving the print invisible, or latent, once again.

Connections

Fingerprints are playing an increasing important role in solving crimes. Once prints are visualized, they must be analyzed. At one time, this process was performed visually by fingerprint experts. Today, prints are scanned and digitally encoded into a computerized program, the Automated Fingerprint Identification Systems (AFIS). Files in AFIS mark ridge details of fingerprints. When fingerprints are compared to others in the database, the marked details are checked at high speed. AFIS has made it possible for forensic investigators to check an unknown print against prints on file all over the world in just a few hours. This technology has made it difficult for criminals to flee from one state to another, or one country to another, to avoid arrest.

 ## Want to Know More?

See appendix for Our Findings.

Further Reading

Chow, Lawrence. "Lifting Fingerprints with Powder and Chemicals," *Forensic Biology*, 2001. Available online. URL: http://www.bxscence.edu/publications/forensics/articles/fingerprinting/f-fing03.htm. Accessed May 19, 2008. This article discusses the effectiveness of using powders and chemicals to lift latent prints.

Cullen, John. "Fingerprint Detection and Recovery," School of Chemical and Pharmaceutical Sciences, Dublin Institute of Technology, 2007. Available online. URL: http://www.heacademy.ac.uk/assets/ps/ fingerprintsDIT.pdf. Accessed May 23, 2008. This Web page provides a short and colorful explanation of methods used in visualizing latent prints.

German, Ed. "Cyanoacrylate (Superglue) Fuming Tips," Onin.com. Available online. URL: http://onin.com/fp/cyanoho.html. Updated August 1, 2003. Accessed June 6, 2008. This Web site gives detailed information on how to carry out cyanoacrylate fuming and offers some troubleshooting tips.

14. Best Solvents for Chromatography

Topic

Common solvents have varied properties that aid in identifying chemicals.

Introduction

The first research paper dealing with *chromatography* was published in 1903. Mikhail Semyonovich Tsvet, an Italian-Russian botanist and chemist (1872–1919), used a tube of solid calcium carbonate to separate the pigments in leafy green plants. This experiment pioneered the basic concept of column chromatography, a solid through which passes a solvent containing the compounds to be separated. The compounds to be separated during chromatography are called *analytes*. The solvent that dissolves the analytes and carries them through the column is called the *effluent* or *mobile phase*.

Chromatography separates analytes in solution by the process of *adsorption,* the attraction of molecules onto a surface. As the solvent and compound pass through the solid, the analytes temporarily adsorb onto the solid surface. Compounds are separated from each other because they spend different amounts of time adsorbed to the solid surface. This time is dependant on the attraction between the analyte and the solvent. The more a compound is attracted, the longer it will take to travel through the column. Generally, this attraction is governed by polarity: oppositely charged particles are attracted to each other. In this experiment you will perform a simplified form of chromatography and evaluate which solvents provide the best results.

 **Time Required**

35 minutes

Materials

- filter paper
- 3 different black ink pens (both permanent and water soluble)
- 5 150-milliliter (ml) beakers
- 5 stirring rods
- stapler
- 20 ml of distilled water
- 20 ml of denatured alcohol (ethyl alcohol)
- 20 ml of isopropyl alcohol
- 20 ml of nail polish remover (with acetone)
- 20 ml of turpentine
- science notebook

Safety Note Some of the solvents used in this experiment are flammable; take care when handling them and other chemicals. Conduct the experiment in a fume hood or where there is plenty of ventilation. Please review and follow the safety guidelines at the beginning of this volume.

Procedure

1. Cut the filter papers into five strips, each approximately 3 inches (in.) (7.6 centimeters [cm]) long.

2. Loop one end of each strip tightly around the middle of each glass stirring rod. Staple the loop closed so that the strip of paper hangs from the stirring rod. The free end of the strip should dangle from the rod when the rod is held horizontally.

3. Select one of the black ink pens. On the free end of each piece of filter paper make a heavy black dot. The dot should be placed about 0.25 in. (0.6 cm) from the bottom edge of the paper.

4. Holding the glass rod horizontally, place it across the top of the beaker so the free end of the filter paper is suspended inside the

beaker (see Figure 1). Carefully pour one of the solvents into the beaker. The solvent in the beaker should be deep enough to touch the bottom of the paper but not deep enough to submerge the black dot. Repeat this process with the other four rods, beakers and solvents.

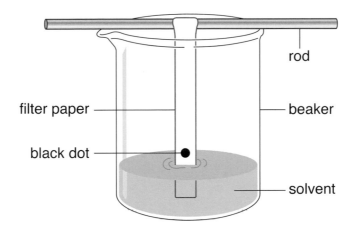

Figure 1

5. Watch as the liquids are drawn up each piece of filter paper through *capillary action*. Notice which solvent(s) is able to dissolve the ink and carry it up the paper.

6. Repeat steps 1 through 5 with the other two pens.

Analysis

1. Which solvent was best able to dissolve the ink in each pen?
2. Rank the solvents used in order from most to least polar.
3. What happens when you used water as a solvent with permanent pen(s)? Why?
4. When the ink separates, which colors move the highest up the strip of filter paper? Why?
5. What causes the colors to separate from each other?

What's Going On?

In this experiment, five different solvents were used to test three different inks. Each solvent moved up the filter paper by *capillary action*. If the ink dissolved in the solvent, then as the solvent moved up the paper the ink moved with it. As the ink traveled, its different components separated based on their relative weights. Lighter-weight molecules traveled faster and thus further from the source than heavier molecules. Figure 2 shows the components of four different inks that were separated by chromatography.

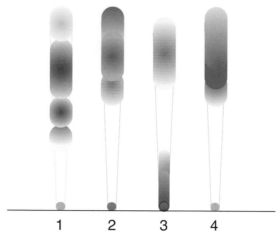

Figure 2

Components of four inks

Solvents tested in the experiment ranged from highly *polar* (water and alcohol) to nonpolar (turpentine). For this experiment the polar solvents were likely the best at dissolving inks, because most inks tend to be either *ionic* or polar. According to the "like dissolves like" rule, the ink spot dissolved in the solvent that is chemically of a similar nature. In other words, a polar solvent dissolved a polar molecule in ink. The nonpolar solvent would have been effective to separate the colors of an organic substance, like the pigments in spinach.

Connections

Chromatography is used extensively in laboratories worldwide because it is one of the best ways to separate a mixture of liquids. When new products are created in a laboratory, they are isolated by chromatography for further study. In forensics, chromatography has many uses. The technique can be employed to test for toxins in water and food sources, to detect explosive material, or to identify unknown drugs found at a crime scene. One very important way that chromatography is used in forensics is *gel electrophoresis*, a type of DNA fingerprinting. For this type of chromatography, a DNA sample replaces the ink dot, and a bed a gel replaces the piece of paper used in this experiment. As an electric current runs through the gel bed, the DNA fragments are drawn up the bed, separating them. Each individual's DNA always makes the same pattern, every time this test is done. In this way, a forensics lab can match the DNA from one sample to another.

 Want to Know More?

See appendix for Our Findings.

Further Reading

Castello, Ana, Mercedes Alvarez, and Fernando Verdu. "DNA From a Keyboard," *Forensic Science Communications*, Volume 6, Number 3, July 2004. Available online. URL: http://www.fbi.gov/hq/lab/fsc/backissu/july2004/case/2004_03_case01.htm. Accessed May 18, 2008. This Web page details a case solved by the use of gel electrophoresis, which is a type of chromatography.

Ramsland, Katherine. "Modern Detection Methods," CrimeLibrary.com, 2007. Available online. URL: http://www.crimelibrary.com/criminal_mind/forensics/toxicology/10.html. Accessed May 18, 2008. This Web site discusses how chromatography is used to identify unknown substances at crime scenes.

Van Blaricum, Ann. "Chromatography," Dogged Research Associates. 1997. Available online. URL: http://www.doggedresearch.com/chromo/chromatography.htm. Accessed May 18, 2008. This Web site accurately explains what chromatography is, how it works, the different types, and how it is used to solve crimes.

15. Using Deductive Reasoning to Solve Crimes

Topic

Criminal investigators turn clues and leads into conclusions through the process of deductive reasoning.

Introduction

Deductive reasoning involves the use of logical and critical thinking to reach a conclusion. Police investigators usually do not learn about the events of a crime in the actual sequence in which they occurred. The evidence and clues are collected in random order. As new evidence becomes available, it is added to the rest of the clues.

Once a large quantity of evidence is collected, criminal investigators begin the process of organizing the clues into their proper sequence. Through deductive reasoning the pieces of the criminal puzzle fall into place and lead to a logical conclusion that can help solve the crime.

Two of the most important skills a criminal investigator needs are the abilities to look and to think. Detectives take detailed notes about things they interpret as being out of place at a crime scene. Witnesses and possible suspects are interviewed. Autopsy results and lab reports are studied. A combination of these actions helps the investigators figure out what the clues mean. In deductive reasoning, a person looks at clues that are available and then draws some conclusions. In this experiment, you will use deductive reasoning to solve a crime.

Time Required

50 to 60 minutes

Materials

- ✏ pencil or pen
- ✏ science notebook

> **Safety Note** Please review and follow the safety guidelines at the beginning of this volume.

Procedure

1. Read the murder case below and take notes about the case in your science notebook.

2. Read and take notes on the crime scene findings, autopsy reports, witness reports, and interviews with possible suspects.

The case:

On May 5th Joe Alexander, the head tennis pro at Lexington Health and Racket Club, was found dead in his office at the club. The assistant coach, Robby Benton, and his wife Jill discovered Joe's body slumped over the racket stringing machine (see Figure 1). Jill screamed in shock, and Bobby immediately used his cell phone to call 911. The night janitor entered the office just minutes after hearing Jill's scream. Records show that the call to the 911 operator was received at 8:28 P.M.

Figure 1

Scene of the crime

Notes from the crime scene:

Police and ambulance arrived at the club at 8:42 P.M. Joe Alexander was pronounced dead at 8:49 P.M. As police investigators carefully surveyed the crime scene, they made the following notes:

- Several strands of racket string were wrapped around Joe's neck.
- Joe's body was draped face down over the racket stinging machine.
- Two blonde hairs and four white hairs were recovered from Joe's clothing.
- Joe's height is 5 feet (ft), 6 inches (in.), and he has dark brown hair.
- Joe is wearing size 8 tennis shoes, white tennis shorts, and a white club T-shirt.
- A red piece of fabric was recovered from a rough edge of the racket stringing machine.
- Joe has a scab over the bridge of his nose and some faint marks that appear to be scratches on his face.
- A set of muddy footprints, men's size 10 or women's size 11, were found on the carpet between the outside door and entrance to Joe's office.

Interview with Joe's employer, Lance Johnson:

- Joe coaches the club's most competitive woman's tennis team.
- The team practices every Thursday night from 6:00 P.M. until 7:00 P.M. at the club and plays matches at 1:00 P.M. on Sunday afternoons at various locations around town.
- There are ten women on the team. The best eight players play each Sunday. The other two members serve as alternates.
- Joe earns additional money by stringing members' rackets on the machine he purchased recently.
- Joe plays in many men's tournaments during the year.

Interview with assistant tennis coach, Robby Benton:

- The regular Thursday night practice was cut short due to a heavy rain. Joe called practice off about 6:20 P.M.
- Of the ten women players, only one player (Mary) missed practice. Mary called just before practice began. She was at the emergency room, where she was being treated for an allergic reaction to a bee sting.

- All the women ran to their cars in the parking lot after the heavy rain began to fall.

- Joe was teaching Robby how to string tennis rackets, and they spent from 6:20 P.M. until 7:35 P.M. in Joe's office restringing rackets. At 7:35 P.M., Jill Benton came by the office and asked if the two of them would like to grab a bite to eat in the club dining room on the upper level. Joe declined the invitation, and Robby Benton and his wife went to the dining room.

- Robby and Jill returned to Joe's office at about 8:28 P.M. The couple saw Joe slumped over the machine. Jill screamed for help while Robby called 911. The scream attracted the attention of the night janitor.

- The office had a distinct odor of musky cologne or perfume when Robby and Jill entered. They thought this was unusual because Joe, Robby, and Jill did not wear any cologne or perfume.

When asked if there were any people that might want to hurt Joe, Robby and Jill provided the following information:

- On the tennis team, eight of the ten players really liked Joe. Two of the women, Nancy and Mary, seemed to dislike him. He had demoted these two women to alternate status and they rarely got to play in matches. Mary asked Joe out recently, but Joe told her he was not interested in dating her.

- Joe was dating Jane Green. Jane was the daughter of Freddie Green, a club member. Freddie had warned Joe sternly several times to stop dating his daughter. Freddie did not like the 10-year age difference between Joe and Jane.

- Last week Joe played in a club tournament and won as usual. In the semifinals he played Dave Jones. He humiliated Dave on the court and laughed each time his serve sped by Dave untouched. After the match, Dave told Joe that he would pay for making him look like a fool in front of everyone.

- Joe had recently strung Gary Morrison's tennis racket. Gary demanded that Joe string it at a very tight tension. Joe warned him that this was too high a tension for Gary's very expensive racket. The next day, Gary's racket cracked while he was playing. Gary stomped into Joe's office and accused Joe of doing shoddy work in stringing the racket. He demanded that Joe buy him a new racket. His racket cost over $500. Joe refused and Gary stormed out of the office.

- The wives of both Ryan Jones and Jeff Turner play on the women's team Joe coaches. On several occasions both of these men have accused Joe of making inappropriate remarks and advances toward their wives. In fact, both have threatened Joe publicly.

Interviews with Tom Sweeny, the night janitor:

- Two or three days ago, Tom overheard Joe on the phone talking to someone about a fight he had gotten into with a club member recently. He did not hear the person's name, but he did hear Joe say the person scratched his face and nose pretty badly and told him he would get worse than that next time.

- Tom reported a strong odor of cologne when he walked into Joe's office the night he was found dead.

- Tom also confirmed the information that Robby and Jill gave police about people who might want to hurt Joe.

- Tom added that he liked Joe okay, but he could be a real show off and hard to deal with sometimes.

Conclusions based on witness interviews:

Police decided that Robby, Jill, and Tom were not suspects since all three had iron-clad alibis for the time of death corroborated by several members in the club.

Autopsy results:

The autopsy results were available the next day and included the following information:

- Cause of death was strangulation. The weapon used was a long piece of tennis string from Joe's stinging machine. Due to the angle of strangulation marks, the murderer was most likely taller than the victim.

- Joe had scratches on his face and nose that were about three days old. They appeared to be inflicted by another person rather than an animal.

- Both white cat hairs and blonde human hairs were found on Joe's body.

- The red fabric taken from the racket stinging machine was confirmed to be nylon. It most likely came from nylon workout shorts.

After officially ruling the case a murder, police established and interviewed a number of suspects. Each suspect denied any involvement in Joe's murder. The following information was obtained from the interviews:

- Ryan, a bank loan officer, and Jeff, a golf instructor, both have wives that played on Joe's tennis team.

- Gary is a veterinarian.

- Only Freddie's shoe size is smaller than men's 10 or women's 11.

- Ryan, Dave, and Freddie wear cologne.

- Gary has a part-time job at the club. He teaches kickboxing class every Thursday night between 7:30 P.M. and 8:45 P.M. He has not missed a class in two years.

- Jeff and Nancy are both 5 ft, 11 in. tall but Mary is 1 in. shorter than Nancy.

- Ryan, Jeff, Gary, and Nancy all have blonde hair.

- Ryan, Freddie, and Nancy own white cats.

- Freddie usually takes a kickboxing class from Gary on Thursday night, but he was not in class this last Thursday night.

- Nancy is a perfume wearer.

- After tennis practice the night of the murder, Nancy headed to the mall, where she works in a men's store. She met a friend at the mall theater. She still had her ticket for the 7:00 P.M. movie showing.

- Mary is allergic to cats and perfume.

- Ryan, Gary, and Dave are graduates of the University of Georgia and are often seen at the gym sporting the Bulldog's red and black colors.

- Dave and Mary have black hair, while Freddie is bald.

- Ryan, Gary, and Dave are all more than 6 ft tall.

- Freddie is three in. shorter than Dave.

- All suspects but Jeff are avid runners and are often seen at the club in running shorts.

- Dave has a hamster, while Jeff is a dog owner.

- Ryan, Jeff, Dave, and Freddie said they were home during the time frame of the murder, but there was no one with them that could corroborate their stories.

- Nancy is a graduate of the University of Florida and hates the color red.

3. The Joe Alexander file is now complete since all evidence has been collected. Using deductive reasoning, figure out who most likely committed this murder. An organized way to assemble your data is to put it all into a logic table. The following table lists the names of the 7 suspects. Each time you find a fact that links that person to the crime, place an X in that box. When you complete the chart, the person with the most X's is your most likely suspect.

Logic Table								
Suspect	**Shoe size fits foot-print**	**Hair color matches human hair evidence**	**Has or has access to white cat**	**Is known to wear nylon running shorts**	**Taller than victim**	**Known to wear the color red**	**Wears cologne or perfume on regular basis**	**Did not give an alibi that could be confirmed by another**
Ryan								
Jeff								
Gary								
Dave								
Freddie								
Nancy								
Mary								

Analysis

1. According to your logic table, who was the most likely murderer?

2. Who was the least likely murderer? Why?

3. Which suspects were able to produce reliable alibis?

4. List the possible motives for each of the seven suspects.

5. What piece of evidence would have disappeared on its own after about an hour or so if a witness had not detected it early on?

6. Do you know for certain that the person you chose as your most likely murderer did indeed commit the crime? Explain your answer.

7. Explain how you used deductive reasoning to solve this crime.

What's Going On?

In this activity you organized crime scene notes and clues into a logical format with the help of a logic table. Through deductive reasoning, you used clues to reach conclusions.

When organizing the clues into the logic table, Ryan had an "X" in every column of the chart making him the most likely murderer. Even though there is much compelling evidence against Ryan, there is still a chance he did not commit the crime. But the large amount of evidence would indicate to investigators that an in-depth investigation of Ryan needs to take place.

All of the suspects in this case had a motive for the murder but only a few had an iron-clad alibi. Gary was busy teaching his kick boxing class, Mary was at the emergency room suffering from a bee sting, and Nancy had proof she was at the movies. The other four suspects had no one to corroborate their whereabouts during the time frame of the murder.

Connections

Sherlock Holmes, Sir Arthur Conan Doyle's fictional detective, was a master of logical thinking. He solved problems by working backwards from the result to the cause by collecting evidence and clues that would eventually lead to the solution of the mystery.

In Doyle's many books, Sherlock Holmes read the evidence and used logic and deductive reasoning to determine what it meant. He also had an innate ability to discern significant from insignificant evidence. In the book, *The Reigate Puzzle*, Holmes states, "It is a highest importance in the art of detection to be able to recognize, out of a number of facts, which are incidental and which are vital. Otherwise your energy and attention must be dissipated instead of being concentrated."

In more than one of Doyle's books, Holmes is accused by untrained observers of guessing to solve a crime. One of Holmes classic responses is, "When you eliminate the impossible, whatever remains, however improbable, must be the truth." Successful criminal investigators of today share an important characteristic with the fictional Sherlock Holmes; they are adept logical thinkers.

Want to Know More?

See appendix for Our Findings.

Further Reading

Benny, Daniel. "The Uses of Inductive and Deductive Reasoning in Investigations and Criminal Profiling," BECCA. Available online. URL: http://www.becca-online.org/images/Inductive_Reasoning_-_Benny.pdf. Accessed May 23, 2008. Benny discusses the value in reasoning and logic in analyzing information.

Godwin, Maurice. "Brief Discussion on Inductive/Deductive Profiling," Godwin Trial & Forensic Consutancy, Inc., 2006. Available online. URL: http://www.investigativepsych.com/inductive.htm. Accessed May 22, 2008. Dr. Godwin's article is a scientific discussion of the use of inductive and deductive reasoning in solving criminal cases.

Trochim, William M. K. "Deductive and Inductive Thinking," Research Methods Knowledge Base, 2006. Available online. URL: http://www.socialresearchmethods.net/kb/dedind.php. Accessed May 22, 2008. The article on this Web page compares deductive and inductive thought processes and explains how these two forms of reasoning are vital when approaching problems logically.

16. Comparison of Two Presumptive Tests for Blood

Topic

Presumptive tests for blood vary in accuracy and value.

Introduction

At a crime scene, investigators want to know if the stains they encounter are blood. Stains made by blood are so similar to ketchup, paint, or rust that they cannot be distinguished by visual inspection alone. Presumptive blood tests are preliminary tests that indicate if a given stain might be blood. These tests do not determine blood type or differentiate between human and animal blood. However, presumptive blood tests are useful in eliminating some stains.

Two commonly used presumptive tests are the hydrogen-peroxide test and the Kastle-Meyer test. Both analyses are based on the activity of *catalase,* an enzyme found in blood. Catalase speeds up the chemical reaction that changes hydrogen peroxide (H_2O_2) into harmless water and oxygen gas that is released in the form of bubbles. This reaction is represented as follows:

$$2 H_2O_2 \rightarrow 2 H_2O \text{ and } O_2$$

This biochemical reaction is critically important in living things because hydrogen peroxide, which is produced during normal metabolic processes, is a toxic waste product. The breakdown of hydrogen peroxide protects tissues from damage.

A few drops of hydrogen peroxide on a bloodstain immediately trigger the breakdown of hydrogen peroxide. As a result, the stain bubbles profusely, releasing O_2 in the process. For this reason, bubbling is considered to be a positive hydrogen peroxide test for the presence of blood.

A second presumptive check for blood is the Kastle-Meyer test. This type of analysis uses a special solution of phenolphthalein and hydrogen peroxide. Change in color from yellow to bright pink indicates that blood may be present. Figure 1 shows the color of the Kastle-Meyer solution in a positive test. In this experiment, you will compare the effectiveness of the hydrogen peroxide and the Kastle-Meyer presumptive blood tests.

Figure 1

Positive Kastle-Meyer test

Time Required

55 minutes

Materials

- ethanol (in dropper bottle)
- hydrogen peroxide (in dropper bottle)
- Kastle-Meyer solution (in dropper bottle)
- de-ionized water (in dropper bottle)
- 6 cotton swabs
- 2 beef blood stains on cotton fabric
- 5 unknown stains on cotton fabric
- science notebook

Safety Note Wear gloves and goggles when working with chemicals. Please review and follow the safety guideline at the beginning of this volume.

Procedure

1. Perform a positive control test for hydrogen peroxide. To do so:

    a. Dampen the tip of a cotton swab with a little de-ionized water.

    b. Rub the damp cotton swab on one beef blood stain so that you collect some of the blood on the swab.

    c. Apply a few drops of hydrogen peroxide to the blood on the swab.

    d. Observe the reaction between the hydrogen peroxide and blood. Bubbling is a positive presumptive test for blood.

2. Perform a positive control test using the Kastle-Meyer method. To do so:

    a. Dampen the tip of a cotton swab with a little de-ionized water.

    b. Rub the damp cotton swab on the other beef blood stain so that you collect some of the blood on the swab.

    c. Apply a few drops of ethanol to the blood on the swab.

    d. Apply a few drops of the Kastle-Meyer solution to the blood on the swab.

    e. Apply a few drop of hydrogen peroxide to the blood on the swab. The development of a pink color is a positive presumptive test for blood.

3. Test the five unknown stains with hydrogen peroxide to find out if they give a positive test for blood. Record your results on the data table in the column titled "hydrogen peroxide test."

4. Test the five unknown stains with Kastle-Meyer solution to find out if they give a positive test for blood. Record your results on the data table in the column titled "Kastle-Meyer test."

Analysis

1. Why might an investigator need to determine whether or not a stain is made of blood?

2. Describe a positive hydrogen peroxide test.

3. Describe a positive Kastle-Meyer test.

4. What is catalase?

5. A slice of potato gives a positive catalase test. Explain why.

6. Which presumptive test do you prefer, the hydrogen peroxide test or the Kastle-Meyer test? Explain your answer.

Data Table		
	Hydrogen-peroxide test	**Kastle-Meyer test**
Unknown 1		
Unknown 2		
Unknown 3		
Unknown 4		
Unknown 5		

What's Going On?

To assess the relevance of stains found at crime scenes, investigators first determine if the stains might contain blood. Hydrogen peroxide is an easy and inexpensive presumptive blood test that relies on bubbling to indicate catalase, an enzyme found in blood. Despite its advantages, hydrogen peroxide can give a false positive result if it contacts other catalase-containing tissues.

Kastle-Meyer solution, made from phenolphthalein, is pale yellow. To perform the Kastle-Meyer test, the stain is first cleaned in alcohol, a process that increases the sensitively of the stain by exposing *hemoglobin*, a protein in blood. Kastle-Meyer solution is added to the cleaned stain, followed by hydrogen peroxide. Chemically, hydrogen peroxide is basically water with an extra atom of oxygen, which makes the compound extremely reactive. The reaction of hemoglobin with hydrogen peroxide yields electrons which *oxidize* the Kastle-Meyer solution, producing the intense pink color (see Figure 2). Because the Kastle-Meyer test depends on the presence of hemoglobin instead of catalase, it gives a fairly reliable presumptive blood test.

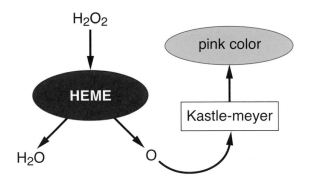

Figure 2

Connections

A good presumptive blood test is one that uses only small portions of the bloodstains in question and therefore does not destroy the evidence for further analysis. Other presumptive blood tests include benzidine, o-tolidine, tetramethylbenzidine (TMB), and leucomalachite green (LMG). Benzidine and O-tolidine are chemically similar tests. Both produce a blue color when they come in contact with blood. However, an essential ingredient in these tests can cause cancer, so they are rarely used. A safer test is TMB, which produces a green to blue-green color. LMG yields a green positive test, but is not as accurate as TMB.

Other chemical tests for blood are chemiluminescence, fluorescence, luminal, and fluorescein. Blood is visualized in these tests as a glowing color. Immediately after bloodstains are visualized, they are photographed or videotaped. Advantages of the glowing tests are a high level of accuracy and sensitivity. Even old blood and blood that has been cleaned from surfaces will still give a positive test. On the downside, these four tests damage the evidence and prevent further testing.

 ## Want to Know More?

See appendix for Our Findings.

Further Reading

Jones, Kristina. "How to Detect Fingerprints and Blood at a Crime Scene, Field Reagent Tests," *Associated Content*, December 30, 2006. Available online. URL: http://www.associatedcontent.com/article/109258/how_to_detect_fingerprints_and_blood.html. Accessed May 10, 2008. Jones, a criminologist, shares her opinions on blood tests that can be used in the field during criminal investigations.

Ramsland, Catherine. "Serology," CrimeLibrary.com. 2007. Available online. URL: http://www.crimelibrary.com/criminal_mind/forensics/serology/3.html. Accessed May 10, 2008. This Web page provides an accurate and easy-to-read overview of presumptive blood tests.

Schiro, George. "Collection and Preservation of Blood Evidence from Crime Scenes." Available online. URL: http://www.crime-scene-investigator.net/blood.html. Accessed May 8, 2008. Schiro, who works with the Louisiana State Police Crime Laboratory, reviews the use and chemistry of several types of serological tests.

17. Lead Poisoning From Dishware

Topic

Dishware can contain enough lead to be a source of accidental poisoning.

Introduction

Lead has been mined since about 6000 B.C.E. This heavy metal is prized for its easy workability and resistance to corrosion. However, lead presents a serious health threat. Lead poisoning can cause many problems, particularly in young children. When lead enters the bloodstream, the metal binds to important *enzymes*, chemicals that speed up biochemical reactions. These enzymes combine with lead because it is similar to several metals that the body needs, such as calcium and iron. However, once tied up with lead, the enzymes cannot perform their normal jobs, which involve body functions from digestion to neurological processes. As a result, the effects of lead poisoning are highly varied and widespread throughout the body. Some of the health problems caused by lead include neurological issues such as hyperactivity, insomnia, learning disabilities, or even seizures and coma. Digestive problems can range from vomiting to poor appetite and extreme weight loss. In small children, the effects are even more damaging because the metal prevents some systems in the body from developing fully or properly.

In modern times, most people are aware of the dangers of lead, and those who are exposed encounter the metal unknowingly. The most common source of lead poisoning in the United States comes from the inhalation or ingestion of lead-based tints used in wall paint, in dishware, or in the manufacture of toys. In recent years, some toys have been recalled because of the possibility of lead in the paint (see Figure 1).

The identification of lead in paint is critically important. Many companies make and distribute lead detection kits that use an *oxidation-reduction reaction* to create the lead *ion*. The ion reacts to change the color of an *indicator*. In this experiment you will test several pieces of dishware to detect the presence of lead.

Figure 1

Recalled toy

Time Required

35 minutes

Materials

- 50 milliliters (ml) of 2.0 molar (M) rhodizonic acid sodium solution (sodium rhodizonate)
- 3 samples of different dishware
- sterile cotton swabs
- 200 ml of white vinegar
- paper towels
- science notebook

Safety Note   Wear goggles and gloves when working with chemicals. Be careful not to touch the tips of the cotton swabs with your fingers as you will contaminate them. Please review and follow the safety guidelines at the beginning of this volume.

Procedure

1. Examine your three pieces of dishware. Make a prediction as to whether or not they contain lead paint. Record your predictions on the data table.

2. Wet a paper towel with the white vinegar. Wipe one piece of dishware with the vinegar. Be careful to apply an even coat of vinegar on the dish.

3. Dip a cotton swab into the rhodizonic acid sodium solution. Rub the dish with the moist swab. A change in color to red indicates the presence of lead. Record your observation on the data table.

4. Repeat steps 2 and 3 with each piece of dishware.

5. Dispose of all cotton swabs and paper towels in the appropriate containers.

Data Table		
	Prediction	**Observation**
Sample 1		
Sample 2		
Sample 3		

Analysis

1. Were your predictions correct or incorrect? Explain the reasoning behind each prediction.

2. What do you think is the purpose of the vinegar in this experiment?

3. Why did you have to be careful not to contaminate the cotton swabs?

4. What might have happened if contamination did occur?

5. What might happen if you served your family dinner on the dishware that contained lead?

What's Going On?

When a surface that contains lead is swabbed with vinegar, lead ions (Pb^{+2}) form. These ions are produced because electrons leave the lead atoms, creating particles with positive charges. When you expose lead ions (which are now short of electrons) to the electron-rich rhodizonic acid sodium solution, an *oxidation-reduction reaction* takes place. In this reaction, the rhodizonic acid sodium solution and the lead ions are attracted to each other. The resulting complex of atoms is highly colored. Contamination is a concern with this experiment because there are many sources of environmental lead that we are exposed to everyday. If you touch the dish (or another source of lead) and then touch the swab, you may cause a false positive result.

Connections

While there have been many efforts to eliminate sources of lead from our everyday lives, lead poisoning still remains a very real health problem, particularly for children. Adults and children are exposed to the same amounts of lead. However, children are more apt to put items in their mouths, so are more likely to ingest the lead dust. In addition, the body systems of adults have already developed fully. To reduce lead poisoning, many sources of lead have been eliminated or reduced from the environment. In the mid 1970s, the first scientific studies linked lead poisoning to lead additives in gasoline. Lead reduces engine problems and makes cars run more smoothly. The studies prompted a reduction in the amount of lead in gasoline and manufacturers were forced to find alternative additives. Since 1996, all gasoline has been lead-free.

Lead has been used as a pigment in house paint for centuries. In fact, houses built before 1978 may still contain lead-based paint. When an older house is renovated, lead dust can be liberated and inhaled. Paint with more than 0.06 percent lead was banned in 1978, and all house paint manufactured since then is substantially free of lead.

Lead is still used in decorative dishes like those shown in Figure 2. Lead glaze yields a smooth, glasslike finish that permits the colors of undercoats to shine through. In addition, lead glaze provides strength and prevents moisture from infiltrating the paints. Many artists prefer lead glazes over other types because of these advantages. Food placed in lead-glazed dishes can absorb the lead. If you suspect that your dishware may contain lead, take precautions. Avoid putting highly acidic foods on the dishes, do not heat food in the dishes, and do not store food in the dishes. To be completely safe, test the dishes for lead and if they are positive, do not use them to prepare or serve food.

Figure 2

Dishware with lead glaze

Want to Know More?

See appendix for Our Findings.

Further Reading

Lead Based Paint Hazard Prevention Program. "Lead Poisoning Prevention," 2007. Available online. URL: http://www.vhcb.org/Lead/leadpoisoning.html. Accessed May 12, 2008. Ways to avoid exposure to common sources of lead poisoning are described.

Science News. "Lead in the Environment causes Violent Crime," ScienceDaily, February 26, 2005. Available online. URL: http://www.sciencedaily.com/releases/2005/02/050223145108.htm. Accessed May 12, 2008. This Web site discusses research that has linked lead poisoning to the occurrence of violent crime.

Washington State Department of Health. "Effects of Lead Poisoning." Updated January 25, 3008. Available online. URL: http://www.doh.wa.gov/ehp/Lead/effects.htm. Accessed May 12, 2008. This Web site describes the effects of lead poisoning on adults and children.

18. Glitter As Trace Evidence

Topic

Glitter as trace evidence collected from victims and suspects can be characterized and used to establish associations.

Introduction

When two people make physical contact, each one picks up something and leaves behind something. If the contact is a criminal matter, the materials transferred are considered to be *trace evidence*. Some types of trace evidence include hair, fibers, particles of soil, paint chips, glass chips, and gunpowder residue. Much trace evidence is minute and almost invisible to the casual observer. Glitter is one type of trace evidence that can be valuable in solving a crime.

Glitter is found in many cosmetic products such as powder, blush, lipstick, and eye shadow. In addition, glitter is applied "on top of" other cosmetics to give extra shimmer. Glitter has hundreds of other uses: for example, it is popular in arts and crafts in paints, beads, candles, and stamps. Glitter is also incorporated into textiles, in some lines of clothing, and in fashion accessories. Decorators and florists can use glitter in fresh or dried floral arrangements. Toys, ornaments, plastics, and paints contain glitter. In this experiment, you will examine glitter from several sources to find out if glitter can be characterized.

Time Required

55 minutes

Materials

- 5 samples of glitter from known sources
- sample of glitter from the "crime scene"
- microscope

- microscope slide
- microscope slide cover slip
- dropper bottle of water
- forceps
- small, transparent metric ruler
- science notebook

Safety Note   Please review and follow the safety guidelines at the beginning of this volume.

Procedure

1. Make a wet mount slide of glitter sample 1. To do so:
    a. Pick up a few pieces of glitter with forceps.
    b. Place the glitter on a microscope slide.
    c. Put a drop of water on the glitter, then cover the water and glitter with a cover slip (see Figure 1).

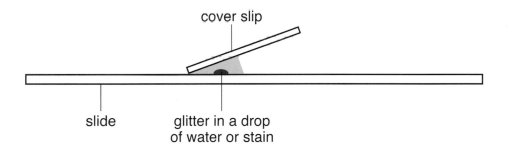

cover slip

slide   glitter in a drop of water or stain

Figure 1

2. Examine the slide under the microscope. To do so:
    a. Place the slide on the microscope stage and focus on low power.
    b. Switch to medium power and focus again.
3. Record the color of the glitter on the data table.
4. Describe or sketch the shape of the glitter on the data table.

5. Place the transparent ruler onto the slide near a piece of glitter. Each line on the ruler represents a millimeter. Estimate the size of one piece of glitter and record the size on the data table.

6. Repeat steps 1 through 5 with the other 4 samples of glitter.

7. Repeat steps 1 through 5 with the glitter from the "crime scene."

Data Table			
	Color	**Shape**	**Size**
Sample 1			
Sample 2			
Sample 3			
Sample 4			
Sample 5			
Crime scene sample			

Analysis

1. What is trace evidence?

2. Ideal trace evidence has the following characteristics:

   a. Nearly invisible

   b. Easily transferred

   c. Highly individualistic

   d. Easily collected

   In your opinion, which of these characteristics describes glitter? Explain your reasoning.

3. Suggest another experiment that you could perform on glitter from a crime scene to help single it out for identification.

4. In your opinion, could glitter be used to link a suspect to a crime scene? Explain your answer.

What's Going On?

Every person who is physically involved in a crime leaves some trace of his or her presence and picks up some trace of another's presence from the crime scene. Ideal trace evidence is highly individualistic and can be tracked to one source. Although glitter may not meet the standards of "ideal," it comes close. During its manufacture, glitter is produced by a stamping machine that cuts large sheets of foil into tiny pieces. Different manufacturers cut their glitter into different sizes. At least 10 different sizes of glitter have been identified. In addition, not all pieces of glitter have the same shape (see Figure 2). Some pieces are square, while others are hexagonal or triangular. The thickness of glitter varies also, depending on whether a single or multiple layers of material were stamped. Because the sheets of unstamped glitter are made of different materials, the density of glitter particles may vary. All of these variations means that not all glitter is the same, and glitter found at a crime scene might be matched to glitter found on a suspect.

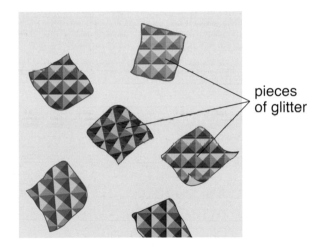

pieces
of glitter

Figure 2

Connections

Glitter has been critical in solving some difficult cases. In Missouri, Travis Glass was convicted of the murder of a thirteen-year old girl. Glitter provided strong supporting evidence in this case. Glass was employed by the victim's father as a bartender. The victim and Glass had met on a few occasions at the bar and at the victim's home. One evening, the victim was at home alone while her parents were at work and her younger siblings were at the sitter's house. When the victim's mother returned from work, her daughter was missing. The police were called in, and a search was instigated. Neighbors reported seeing Glass' car at the victim's home late that night. Glass was picked up and interviewed and his car and home searched. Crime scene investigators examined trace evidence on Glass' clothing and car and found bits of glitter. The glitter proved to be identical to glitter in the body spray that belonged to the victim.

Want to Know More?

See appendix for Our Findings.

Further Reading

Blackledge, Bob. "Glitter as Forensic Evidence," National Forensic Science Center. Available online. URL: http://nfstc.org/projects/trace/docs/final/Blackledge_Glitter.pdf. Accessed May 22, 2008. Blackledge, a retired criminologist, discusses the varieties of glitter and how they can be a valuable type of trace evidence in solving criminal cases.

Jones, Allison, "Forensic Handbook 2—Trace Evidence," *Science in Society*, May 2002. Available online. URL: http://www.channel4.com/science/microsites/S/science/society/forensic_trace.html. Accessed May 23, 2008. Written in layman's terms, this Web site describes different types of trace evidence.

Michigan State Police. "Trace Evidence," 2008. Available online. URL: http://www.michigan.gov/msp/0,1607,7-123-1593_3800-15961–,00.html. Accessed May 22, 2008. The Michigan State Police trace evidence Web site discusses different types of possible trace evidence and how this evidence can be valuable in solving a variety of crimes.

19. Rate of Cooling

Topic

The environment affects the rate at which a decedent's body cools.

Introduction

The determination of the time of death of a *decedent* can rarely be made with complete accuracy. Time of death is usually an estimate. Chemical changes that occur in the human body after death can help make this determination. These changes include the degree of rigidity or *rigor mortis*, the degree of discoloration in the tissues or *livor mortis*, and body temperature or *algor mortis*. In life, body temperature is about 98.6 degrees Fahrenheit (°F) (37 degrees Celsius [°C]). Once death occurs, the body begins to cool until it reaches the temperature of the environment. For this reason, an investigator needs to know the temperature of the body as well as the temperature of the environment. By knowing how fast a body cools every hour, a determination of time of death can be estimated. If the *post mortem interval*, the time between death and examination of the body, is short, the estimate of time of death can be made with a fair degree of accuracy. Once the body reaches the same temperature as the environment, this technique is no longer helpful. In this experiment, you will devise a procedure to compare the rates at which tissue cools in the air and in water.

Time Required

55 minutes

Materials

- 2 small uncooked chicken wings
- 2 thermometers
- 1 gallon-size plastic bag

- hot pad
- paper plate
- 400-milliliter (ml) beaker of water
- clock
- graph paper
- gloves
- science notebook

Safety Note   Take care when working with raw chicken. Wear gloves and wash you hands and everything that comes in contact with the raw chicken. Please review and follow the safety guidelines at the beginning of this volume.

Procedure

1. Your job is to design and perform an experiment to compare the rate at which tissue cools in air and in water.

2. You can use any of the supplies provided by your teacher, but you will not need to use all of them. If you would like to use additional supplies, consult your teacher to see if they are available.

3. Before you conduct your experiment, decide exactly what you are going to do. Write the steps you plan to take (your experimental procedure) and the materials you plan to use (materials list) on the data table. Show your procedure and materials list to the teacher. If you get teacher approval, proceed with your experiment. If not, modify your work and show it to your teacher again.

4. As you design your experiment, keep these points in mind:

   a. Control all variables. In this experiment, you want to compare the rate at which the tissue in a chicken wing cools when the wing is exposed to the air and when the wing is underwater. Keep all other variables the same. Variables include, but are not limited to, the size of the chicken wing, the starting temperature of the air and water, and the location in which the experiment is performed.

   b. Carry out more than one trial in your experiment.

     c. Keep accurate records as you do your experiment. Records can include descriptions, measurements, and drawings. When appropriate, record the data you collect in data tables and display the data on graphs.

5. Once you have teacher approval, assemble the materials you need and begin your procedure.

Data Table	
Your experimental procedure	
Your materials list	
Teacher's approval	

Analysis

1. Which do you think will cool faster, a small body or a large one? Explain your answer.

2. Based on your experimental results, under which conditions does tissue cool fastest—in air or in water? Why do you think this is so?

3. How do you think the presence of clothing would affect the rate of cooling? Explain your answer.

4. How do you think wind would affect the rate of cooling? Explain your answer.

5. Based on your experimental results, at what rate does the tissue of a chicken exposed to the air cool each hour? How much does tissue in water cool each hour?

What's Going On?

According to the English physicist Sir Isaac Newton (1642–1727), the rate at which a small, inorganic material cools is determined by the difference in the temperature of the material and the environment. A graph showing the change in a material's temperature plotted against time produces a descending exponential curve (see Figure 1). However, this relationship between time and temperature does not transfer directly to a human body, which is made up of a variety of organic materials along with a large proportion of water. Another factor in body cooling is that humans have a relatively large surface area and an irregular shape. A graph showing the cooling of a body yields an S-shaped curve (see Figure 2). At first, the body temperature drops slowly, but after some time the rate of cooling becomes more linear. As the body temperature reaches that of the environment, cooling slows once again.

As a rule of thumb, a body (exposed to air) begins to cool at a rate of 1° to 1.5°F per hour until it reaches the temperature of the environment. A simple formula reflects this rule:

approximate hours since death = 98.6°F – body temperature ÷ 1.5

Several factors have to be considered in this calculation. In cold weather, cooling occurs more quickly than in warm weather. In addition, a large person does not cool as quickly as a small one. Clothing can insulate the body and slow cooling. In some cases, the body temperature was unusually high just before death due to drugs or illness. A body cools faster in water than air because water is a good conductor that moves heat

Change in temperature of material over time

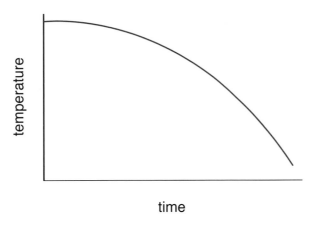

Figure 1

Change in temperature of human body over time

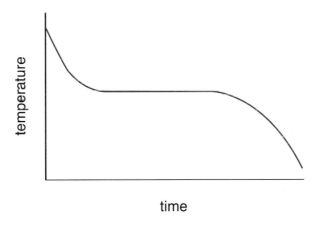

Figure 2

away from the body. Generally, cooling in still water is about twice as fast as in still air. In moving water, a body cools about three times as rapidly.

Connections

When a decedent is found at a crime scene, one of the first tasks is to determine body temperature. One case that was partially solved by analysis of body temperature was the unexplained death of actor and comedian, John Belushi. Belushi was found dead in his home at 12:35 A.M. At that time, Belushi's body was showing some rigidity and changes in skin color that suggested that he died between 8:30 and 10:30 P.M. the previous evening. However, body temperature did not confirm these estimates. Body temperature, which was taken four hours after his body was discovered, was found to be 95°F. Based on body temperature alone, one might believe that his death had occurred as late as 1:00 A.M., which was impossible. To explain this discrepancy, pathologists concluded that Belushi's body temperature at time of death must have been highly elevated. Factors that can elevate body temperature include certain diseases and drugs. Eventually, a confession by a friend, Cathy Smith, cleared the mystery. She admitted to giving Belushi an injection of cocaine and heroin about 8:30 P.M. on the evening before his death. This combination of drugs would have elevated his body temperature several degrees higher than normal just before his death. For her role in his death, Smith was convicted of involuntary manslaughter.

 Want to Know More?

See appendix for Our Findings.

Further Reading

East Tennessee State University. "ETSU researchers use CIE procedure to determine time of death," February 2001. Available online. URL: http://www.etsu.edu/etsu/news/20010027.htm. Accessed May 22, 2008. This article explains a new technique for determining time of death.

Pounder, Derrick J. "Postmortem Changes and Time of Death," Department of Forensic Medicine, University of Dundee. Available online. URL: http://www.dundee.ac.uk/forensicmedicine/notes/timedeath.pdf. Accessed May 22, 2008. These detailed lecture notes explain several methods for determining time of death.

Staerkeby, Morten. "What Is Forensic Entomology?" *Entomology*. Available online. URL: http://www.kathyreichs.com/entomology.htm. Accessed May 12, 2008. This Web page provides an excellent description of how to use insects to help determine time of death.

20. Cross Section of Textile Fibers

Topic

Cross section analysis can help identify fibers.

Introduction

When two people come into contact, there is the chance that fibers will be transferred from one to the other. In forensics, fibers are one type of *trace evidence*, small amounts of materials such as fibers, paint, hair, and chips of paint or glass. A fiber is the smallest unit of a textile, a woven material such as fabric. Fibers can come from plants or animals, or they can be man-made. Cotton, a plant product, is one of the most common fibers in the textile industry. Wool, the hair of sheep, has been used for centuries in garments, blankets, and carpets.

Man-made fibers can be produced from synthetic or processed natural materials. The characteristics of a man-made fiber are partially due to its cross section shape. The cross section of a fiber can be viewed by cutting it at a right angle to the fiber's length. In this experiment, you will prepare slides of cross sections of fibers, examine the fibers, and compare them to a fiber found at a "crime scene."

Time Required

55 minutes

Materials

- small block of paraffin (about 2 inch [in.] by 2 in.) (5 centimeters [cm] by 5 cm)
- 6 small paper or wax cups
- 5 unknown textile fibers (all the same color)
- textile fiber from the "crime scene"

- hot plate
- large beaker
- small beaker
- beaker tongs
- microscope
- scalpel or razor
- 6 microscope slides
- scissors
- masking tape or labels
- toothpicks or straws
- access to water
- science notebook

Safety Note Take care when working with the hot plate, hot water, and hot paraffin. Paraffin is flammable at high temperatures so do not let it come in contact with the hot plate. Take care when working with the scalpel or razor. Please review and follow the safety guidelines at the beginning of this volume.

Procedure

1. Use masking tape or labels to mark the cups as "A," "B," "C," "D," "E," and "Crime Scene."

2. Clip fiber A into several small pieces and place the pieces in cup A.

3. Repeat step 2 for the remaining fibers and cups.

4. Prepare a hot water bath to melt the paraffin by filling the large beaker halfway with water and placing it on the hot plate. Place the paraffin in the small beaker, then use the beaker tongs to insert the small beaker into the large one. Hold the small beaker in the hot water bath until the paraffin melts.

5. Pour a little paraffin into each labeled cup.

6. Use toothpicks or straws to submerge the pieces of fiber under the melted paraffin.

7. Let the paraffin cool for a few minutes.

8. Remove the paraffin from cup A. Use the scalpel or razor to make several very thin slices of paraffin, taking care to include a fiber in each slice. Slices should be so thin that they are almost transparent.

9. Place a few slivers of paraffin that contain fibers on a microscope slide. Carefully position the slide on the microscope stage. Focus first on low power, then on medium.

10. Scan the slide to find a place where a cross section of a fiber can be seen. Draw the cross section shape of this fiber in your science notebook.

11. Repeat steps 8 through 10 for the other cups of fibers and paraffin.

12. Compare the "Crime Scene" fiber with fibers A, B, C, D, and E. Determine which of the fibers is identical to the crime scene fiber.

Analysis

1. Why are fibers considered to be trace evidence?

2. Did all of the fibers have the same shape? Why or why not?

3. Forensic experts are not usually concerned about the cross section shapes of wool or cotton fibers. Explain why.

4. Were you able to match the shape of the fiber from the crime scene to any of the fibers labeled A through E? If so, which one matched?

5. How can viewing the cross section of a fiber be helpful in an investigation?

What's Going On?

The shapes of synthetic fibers depend on the machinery used to produce them. Fiber manufacture begins with a melted *polymer*, a long molecule that is made of smaller units. The liquid polymer is forced through a narrow tube or spinneret, then air dried to produce the fiber (see Figure 1). Polyester, rayon, nylon, and acetate are some man-made fibers.

In forensics, fibers can be characterized in a number of ways to link a suspect to a particular victim or crime scene. A compound light microscopic reveals color as well as the striations and pitting that mark the surfaces of fibers. Analysis with a light infrared spectrophotometer reveals the chemical composition of fibers. *Chromatography* shows the dyes that are used to produce fiber color.

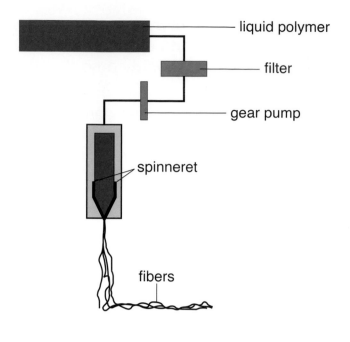

Figure 1

Cross section analysis of fibers reveals their shapes. Several fiber shapes are shown in Figure 2. The most common cross section shape is round because it is easiest to produce and least expensive. Fibers that are produced in a trilobal structure look like three-pointed stars. This shape enables fibers to reflect light, yielding products that stay attractive because they do not show dirt easily. Ribbon-shaped fibers are flattened and highly reflective, so they give sparkle to fabrics. Fibers with bow tie shapes are stretchy and have high resilience.

Connections

The murder of a young Ohio woman was solved with the help of cross-section fiber analysis. The victim's body was abandoned in a field about 30 miles from her home. At the crime scene, investigators discovered a few orange fibers in her hair. Analysis of the fibers showed that they were unusual in both color and shape. Research by the investigators proved that similar fibers had been found on a girl who had been murdered in the same area eight months earlier. This fiber evidence was important, but did not lead directly to a suspect.

Several months after the murder, a young woman escaped from a kidnapper and fled to the police. She described her assailant and his van, which she said had old orange carpet in the back. Investigators located

Fiber shapes

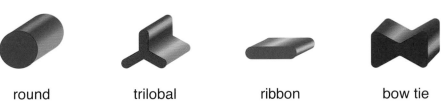

round   trilobal   ribbon   bow tie

Figure 2

the man, examined his van and took carpet samples. The color and shape of fibers in his carpet matched the fibers on the earlier murder victims. Although the carpet had been mass produced in the United States, only 75 yards of it had been shipped to this region of Ohio. The scarcity of this carpet made it unusual and provided a strong link between the van driver and the murder victims, helping to seal his conviction.

Want to Know More?

See appendix for Our Findings.

Further Reading

American Fiber Manufacturers Association, Inc. "Fiberworld Classroom." Available online. URL: http://www.fiberworld.com/. Accessed May 28, 2008. This site provides information on the history, uses, and manufacture of fiber.

Deedrick, Douglas W. "Hairs, Fibers, Crime, and Evidence," *Forensic Science Communications*, Volume 2, Number 3, July 2000. Available online. URL: http://www.fbi.gov/hq/lab/fsc/backissu/july2000/deedric3.htm. Accessed May 27, 2008. Published by the U.S. Department of Justice, this article gives a concise explanation of the value of fiber evidence.

Hanson, Doug. "Fiber Evidence, Animal, Vegetable or Man-made. Not All Fibers Are Alike." Officer.com. January 14, 2008. Available online. URL: http://www.officer.com/web/online/Investigation/Fiber-Evidence/18$39503. Accessed May 28, 2008. Dr. Hanson explains the value of fiber evidence and the types of information that can be gathered from fibers.

Scope and Sequence Chart

This chart aligns the experiments in this book with some of the National Science Content Standards. (These experiments do not address every national science standard.) Please refer to your local and state content standards for additional information. As always, adult supervision is recommended and discretion should be used in selecting an experiment appropriate to teach age group or to individual students.

Standard	Grades 5–8	Grades 9–12
Physical Science		
Properties and changes of properties in matter	2, 3, 9, 11, 14, 15, 20	2, 3, 9, 11, 14, 15, 20
Chemical reactions	2, 3, 14, 15, 16	2, 3, 14, 15, 16
Motions and forces	8	8
Transfer of energy and interactions of energy and matter	1, 4, 8, 12, 19	1, 4, 8, 12, 19
Conservation of energy and increase in disorder	4	4
Life Science		
Cells and structure and function in living systems	1, 2, 5, 6, 13, 15, 16	1, 2, 5, 6, 13, 15, 16
Reproduction and heredity	5, 6	5, 6
Regulation and behavior	16	16

Populations and ecosystems		
Diversity and adaptations of organisms		
Interdependence of organisms		
Matter, energy, and organization in living systems		
Biological evolution		
Earth Science		
Structure and energy in the Earth system	3, 10	3, 10
Geochemical cycles		
Origin and evolution of the Earth system		
Origin and evolution of the universe		
Earth in the solar system		
Nature of Science		
Science in history	14, 17	14, 17
Science as an endeavor	all	all

Grade Level

Title of Experiment	Grade Level
1. Banana Autopsy	6–12
2. Characterization of Types of Carbohydrates	9–12
3. Techniques in Making Shoe Impressions	6–12
4. Dating With Radioactive Isotopes	6–12
5. Mitochondrial DNA	9–12
6. Gel Electrophoresis in DNA Fingerprinting	9–12
7. Probative Value of Class Evidence	6–12
8. Blood Spatter Inquiry	6–12
9. Specific Gravity of Body Fluids	6–12
10. Soil Identification	6–12
11. Density of Glass	6–12
12. Emission Spectra Can Identify Elements	6–12
13. Comparing Latent Fingerprint Techniques	6–12
14. Best Solvents for Chromatography	6–12
15. Using Deductive Reasoning to Solve Crimes	6–12
16. Comparison of Two Presumptive Tests for Blood	6–12
17. Lead Poisoning From Dishware	6–12
18. Glitter As Trace Evidence	6–12
19. Rate of Cooling	6–12
20. Cross Section of Textile Fibers	6–12

Setting

The experiments are classified by materials and equipment use as follows:

- Those under SCHOOL LABORATORY involve materials and equipment found only in science laboratories. Those under SCHOOL LABORATORY must be carried out there.

- Those under HOME involve household or everyday materials. Some of these can be done at home, but call for supervision.

- The experiments classified under OUTDOORS may be done at the school or at the home, but call for supervision.

SCHOOL LABORATORY

2. Characterization of Types of Carbohydrates

6. Gel Electrophoresis in DNA Fingerprinting

9. Specific Gravity of Body Fluids

11. Density of Glass

12. Emission Spectra Can Identify Elements

13. Comparing Latent Fingerprint Techniques

14. Best Solvents for Chromatography

16. Comparison of Two Presumptive Tests for Blood

17. Lead Poisoning From Dishware

18. Glitter As Trace Evidence

20. Cross Section of Textile Fibers

HOME

1. Banana Autopsy

4. Dating With Radioactive Isotopes

5. Mitochondrial DNA

7. Probative Value of Class Evidence

8. Blood Spatter Inquiry

10. Soil Identification

15. Using Deductive Reasoning to Solve Crimes

19. Rate of Cooling

OUTDOORS

3. Techniques in Making Shoe Impressions

Our Findings

1. BANANA AUTOPSY

Idea for class discussion: Ask students to suggest definitions of the term "autopsy." Make a list of the reasons that an autopsy might be needed.

Notes to the teacher: Prepare the banana "victims" before the day of the lab. This preparation can be simple or elaborate, depending on your style. You can dress up the bananas to give them simple outfits, or you can leave them "naked." To add trace evidence, roll some bananas in soil, pet hair, grass, dust, or other materials. You may want to make each banana victim's cause of death unique. Some suggestions include "head" trauma, stab wounds and internal bleeding (insert red candies or a little ketchup with a hypodermic needle). Be creative and make the lab fun as well as informative.

Remind students that some directions in the procedure are a bit tongue-in-cheek. For example, there is no actual shoulder region or pubis, no skull or stomach on a banana victim. However, students are generally not bothered by these discrepancies and find the lab instructive.

Analysis

1. Answers will vary but could include soil, leaves, grass, or dust.
2. Trace evidence could indicate where a person was located at the time of death or where he or she had been before death.
3. Answers will vary.
4. Identifying markings like scars, tattoos, or moles could be used to help identify an unknown victim. Other marks, such as stab wounds, could provide information about whether or not a struggle took place, the position of the victim, or even whether the perpetrator was left- or right-handed.
5. Answers will vary.
6. Answers will vary.
7. Answers will vary.
8. Answers will vary.

2. CHARACTERIZATION OF TYPES OF CARBOHYDRATES

Idea for class discussion: Ask students to give their own definition of the term "carbohydrate." Have them list some examples of carbohydrates.

Notes to the teacher: You can use 0.125 percent iodine/0.5 percent KI or a dilution of this chemical for iodine (or Lugol's) solution. Powdered carbohydrates and amylase solution can be purchased from science supply houses.

Analysis

1. starch: purple, blue, or black; cellulose: no color change; glycogen: no color change

2. starch

3. starch (evidenced by orange precipitate)

4. Answers will vary but should include some of the steps used in this experiment.

3. TECHNIQUES IN MAKING SHOE IMPRESSIONS

Idea for class discussion: Ask students to suggest some reasons that investigators might want to collect shoe impressions. Review these reasons after the experiment.

Notes to the teacher: Before class, go to an outdoor area where soil is relatively soft. Make enough shoes impressions for each lab group to have two. Alternately, supply lab groups with two shallow pans filled with damp soil so that they can make their own shoe impressions in the classroom.

Analysis

1. Impressions of shoes can link a suspect's shoes to the crime scene, or provide information about a suspect's height and weight.

2. Answers will vary based on student experiences.

3. Dental stone; plaster of paris is eroded and damaged by scrubbing.

4. Dental stone; the particles that make up dental stone produce more details than those in plaster of paris.

5. Answers will vary.

6. Answers will vary. Students might state that a shoe impression can indicate scratches or wear patterns that link the impression to a particular pair of shoes.

7. Answers will vary but could include those shown on completed Figure 3 below.

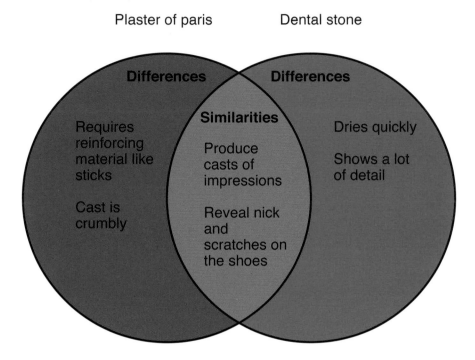

Plaster of paris   Dental stone

Differences   **Differences**

Similarities

Requires reinforcing material like sticks

Produce casts of impressions

Dries quickly

Shows a lot of detail

Cast is crumbly

Reveal nick and scratches on the shoes

Completed Figure 3

4. DATING WITH RADIOACTIVE ISOTOPES

Idea for class discussion: Review the concepts of isotopes and radioactivity. Point out that not all isotopes are radioactive.

Analysis

1. The graph is a slope.

2. Answers will vary.

3. The string became too short to cut.

4. no

5. 2.5 g

6. 150 days

7. 3.125 g

8. Radioactive isotopes that naturally exist in living bone decay at a steady rate that helps scientists determine how long the bone has been dead.

5. MITCHONDRIAL DNA

Idea for class discussion: Many students may not be aware of the fact that mitochondria (and the chloroplasts of plants) contain their own DNA. Explain the endosymbiotic theory of eukaryotic evolution, which states that a host bacterial cell may have engulfed (or been invaded by) another bacterial cell, creating a situation that benefited both. Mitochondria and chloroplasts may have developed from these early guests of the host cells.

Analysis

1. a. same; b. same; c. same; d. different

2. TACTACCCCAAAGGATACGATTCC

3. Answers will vary but could include her father's brother or her fraternal grandparents.

4. a. mother; b. all three children; c. mtDNA

5. See completed Figure 3 below.

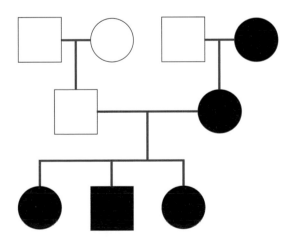

Completed Figure 3

6. No. The DNA of males is carried on a portion of the sperm that does not enter the egg.

7. See completed Figure 4 below.

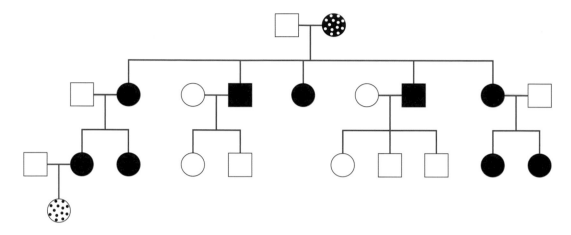

Completed Figure 4

6. GEL ELECTROPHORESIS IN DNA FINGERPRINTING

Idea for class discussion: Ask the class to explain what they already know about a DNA fingerprint and the methods used to prepare it. Post their ideas on the board and review them again after the experiment to see if they can add any information.

Notes to the teacher: You can purchase precut, dyed lambda DNA or entire kits that contain DNA and the materials and directions for preparing agarose gels from science supply houses. If you want to improve the visibility of DNA stains on the gel, you can stain them with a methylene blue.

Analysis

1. Gel electrophoresis makes it possible to analyze the sequence of bases in DNA.

2. The comb creates wells into which DNA samples are injected.

3. The power supply creates an electrical charge that attracts pieces of DNA and pulls them through the gel.

4. Small pieces of DNA move through the gel faster than large ones.

5. The DNA fingerprints in Figure 5 are not exactly alike; they came from different individuals.

6. Answers will vary but students should describe bands of DNA scattered throughout the gel.

7. A DNA fingerprint is a unique banding pattern produced by DNA separated on an agarose gel.

8. Since everyone has a unique DNA fingerprint, DNA from a crime scene can be compared to DNA of a suspect.

9. a. no; b. no; c. no; d. yes. Explanation: the only people who have exactly the same DNA are identical twins.

10. Answers will vary but might be something like the following: prepare agarose gel → inject DNA cut with enzymes → connect power source → let particles of DNA separate on the gel → disconnect power source → analyze bands

7. PROBATIVE VALUE OF CLASS EVIDENCE

Idea for class discussion: Ask students this question: Why are some pieces of evidence more valuable than others? Lead the discussion so students understand that not all evidence provides a strong link between suspect and crime scene or suspect and victim.

Analysis

1. 25 percent

2. 53

3. You need to know the number of female drivers and the number of blue Jeeps in town.

4. Class evidence is associated with a group; individual evidence is only associated with one unique source.

5. See completed Data Table 2 on page 136.

6. By knowing probative value, one can evaluate the usefulness of evidence.

7. Individual evidence came from only one source.

8. Several pieces of class evidence can have high probative value.

Completed Data Table 2

Evidence	Individual or class?	Why?
a. DNA	Individual	The only source is one person.
b. Fingerprint	Individual	The only source is one person.
c. Torn piece of paper	Class	There are many sources of paper.
d. Pair of winter gloves	Class	There are many sources of gloves.
e. Handcuffs	Class	There are many sources of handcuffs.

8. BLOOD SPATTER INQUIRY

Idea for class discussion: Ask students to define blood splatter and discuss its importance in solving a crime.

Analysis

1. Blood spatter helps analyze the crime scene, the position of the victim, the types of injuries on the victim, and the movements of the perpetrator.

2. Target surfaces affect the way blood drops splatter.

3. Answers will vary but could include height from which blood was dropped and angle of the surfaces onto which blood fell.

4. Answers will vary.

5. Answers will vary but could include an experiment to find how the height from which blood was dropped, the angle of target surfaces, or the velocity with which blood drops traveled affects the patterns of blood spatter.

6. The smoother droplet (A) fell on the untextured floor; the droplet with a wavy edge (B) fell on the porous plastic tile. Smooth surfaces offer less surface area to deflect the drop.

9. SPECIFIC GRAVITY OF BODY FLUIDS

Idea for class discussion: Pose the question, "Which weighs more: a pound of feathers or a pound of lead?" Review students' understanding of the terms "weight" and "density." Introduce the concept of specific gravity.

Notes to the teacher: Prepare two blood samples and two urine samples for students to analyze. The blood samples can either be beef blood or something that looks like blood such as dilute ketchup. Put several teaspoons of salt in blood sample 2 so that it will have a higher density than the other sample.

Prepare urine samples by putting a few drops of yellow food color in water. Add several teaspoons of salt to urine sample 2.

Have students pour their 20 ml aliquots from large beakers that you prepare for the class or premeasure each lab group's samples.

Analysis

1. Density is mass per unit volume.
2. No. Density is constant.
3. Answers will vary.
4. Specific gravity is a comparison on the density of a material to the density of water.
5. Blood sample 1 has a lower specific gravity than sample 2 and might have been diluted by water.
6. Urine sample 2 has a higher specific gravity than sample 1 and most likely contains additional proteins and minerals.

10. SOIL IDENTIFICATION

Idea for class discussion: Ask students to define "soil" and list some of the materials that might be found in soil.

Notes to the teacher: Use the same soil for sample B and for the crime scene. Collect three different types of soil before the day of this experiment. Each class of 30 students will need about eight cups of each sample.

Analysis

1. soil sample B

2. Answers will vary but could include color and amount of organic matter.

3. The sieves have different size meshes.

4. Answers will vary. Soil on the victim and soil at the scene of the shooting might be different, suggesting that the victim had been moved.

5. The presence of brick fragments makes the soil unique and helps investigators locate its source.

6. a. 33 percent; b. coastal plain; c. The expert might look for unique materials in the soil that are specific to a certain area.

11. DENSITY OF GLASS

Idea for class discussion: Ask students to brainstorm a list of items that are made of, or contain, glass. Discuss the different uses of glass in these items.

Notes to the teacher: You can use pieces of glass from a variety of sources including beakers or test tubes, lightbulbs, headlights, or leaded glass. Remind students to handle glass with care and use forceps instead of their fingers to pick up pieces.

Analysis

1. The density increases as the sugar is added because the water molecules surround the sugar molecules. Sugar has a much higher density than water.

2. Answers will vary depending on the samples provided.

3. Answers may include disposable or cheaper glassware, or situations in which the weight of the glass needs to be less than usual, such as jewelry or artwork.

4. Answers may include glass that undergoes a great deal of pressure or elevated temperatures. All crystal is dense glass because it contains lead.

5. No. Density is dependant only on the mass and volume of an object. It is a constant physical property.

6. Answers will vary, but should refer to the idea that different glass has different densities and being able to identify where a glass sample originated can be very important.

12. EMISSION SPECTRA CAN IDENTIFY ELEMENTS

Idea for class discussion: Demonstrate to students how a prism breaks light into its component colors. Explain to students that light can be used to identify materials.

Notes to the teacher: Provide about 10 known solutions in which the five unknowns are included. The solutions need to contain a group one or two metals and a fairly nonreactive anion like chloride or nitrate.

Analysis

1. Answers will vary based on the chemicals used.

2. The flame from the Bunsen burner should be the source of energy.

3. The energy is required to cause the electrons to jump to their excited state.

4. Answers will vary but may include contamination, color blindness, mistaking the color of the chemical for the color of the burning cotton swab/wooden splint.

5. Answers will vary.

13. COMPARING LATENT FINGERPRINT TECHNIQUES

Idea for class discussion: Ask students to give their own definitions of fingerprints. Point out that there are fingerprints on many items in the room, but we are not able to see them. Have students suggest some ways to visualize invisible prints.

Analysis

1. Answers will vary. Fingerprints are probably easy to see and deep purple in color.

2. Answers will vary. Fingerprints are probably easy to see and are white.

3. Answers will vary. Superglue and iodine fuming are both generally recommended for nonporous and slightly porous surfaces. See the completed data table on page 140.

4. The iodine prints fade.

5. Answers will vary based on student experimental results.

Completed Data Table		
Material	Iodine fuming	Superglue fuming
Tile	Answers will vary.	Answers will vary.
Glass	Answers will vary.	Answers will vary.
Plastic	Answers will vary.	Answers will vary.
Paper	Answers will vary.	Answers will vary.
Wood	Answers will vary.	Answers will vary.

14. BEST SOLVENTS FOR CHROMATOGRAPHY

Idea for class discussion: Pose this scenario to students: You are an investigator. The only evidence you have in your case is a note written by the perpetrator. What kinds of evidence would investigators be able to get from the note. Help students reach the conclusion that the components of the ink might identify the pen used to write the note.

Analysis

1. Answers will vary depending on the pens used.

2. water, denatured alcohol, isopropyl alcohol, nail polish remover, turpentine

3. Permanent markers will not dissolve in water.

4. The lighter colors will move up the paper the furthest because they have the smallest and lightest weight molecules.

5. Their different weights and sizes. Smaller molecules travel faster and further up the paper, leaving the slower and heavier molecules behind.

15. USING DEDUCTIVE REASONING TO SOLVE CRIMES

Idea for class discussion: Ask students to give examples of occasions when they have used deductive reasoning to solve a problem.

Analysis

1. Ryan

2. Answers will vary.

3. Gary, Mary, and Nancy

4. Ryan believed Joe was flirting with his wife at tennis practice and matches. Gary was angry because his expensive racket cracked after Joe put new strings on it. Freddie's daughter dated Joe, and Freddie thought Joe was too old for his daughter. Mary was angry because she did not get to play in tennis matches; plus, Joe refused to go out with her. Nancy was angry because she never got to play in the tennis matches because Joe demoted her to an alternate. Dave was humiliated by Joe during a public tennis tournament. Jeff thought Joe was flirting with his wife.

5. the odor of the cologne

6. No, because the evidence is circumstantial.

7. In deductive reasoning, a person looks at clues that are available and then draws some conclusions through critical and logical thinking.

16. COMPARISON OF TWO PRESUMPTIVE TESTS FOR BLOOD

Idea for class discussion: Ask students if they have ever seen a movie that involved a lot of blood. Let one or two students explain what they know about this stage blood. Point out that many red substances resemble blood.

Notes to the teacher: Prepare the four unknown stains on cotton fabric by cutting old T-shirts into small squares and staining each square with ketchup, beet juice, rust, or red paint. Alternately, you could also use tomato juice and red food coloring. Do not label these pieces of fabric; they will serve as students' unknowns. Stain two more pieces with beef blood and label them.

Buy a prepared solution of phenophthalin (Kastle-Meyer solution) or prepare it before the lab. Combine 2 g phenolphthalein (powder) with 20 g potassium hydroxide (CAUTION: caustic, strong base) and 100 ml water. Mix thoroughly. Add 20 g powdered zinc. Allow the mixture to sit for 48 hours or until it becomes colorless. Store the mixture in brown bottle or bottle wrapped with foil.

Analysis

1. Investigators need to separate important blood stains from unimportant, incidental stains at the crime scene. Blood at a crime scene suggests that someone is injured and that a serious crime may have occurred.

2. bubbling

3. development of pink color

4. Catalase is an enzyme that breaks down hydrogen peroxide into water and oxygen gas.

5. Many living things produce hydrogen peroxide as a by-product of metabolism as well as catalase to break down the hydrogen peroxide.

6. Answers will vary. The hydrogen peroxide test is easier to carry out, but the Kastle-Meyer test is more accurate.

17. LEAD POISONING FROM DISHWARE

Idea for class discussion: Find out what students know about lead and other heavy metals. If possible, point out the heavy metals on the periodic table and discuss their chemical and physical characteristics.

Notes to the teacher: Collect some dishes that are decorative and not intended for food. These are more likely to contain lead.

Analysis

1. Answers will vary.

2. The vinegar is used to produce the lead ion from the lead atom.

3. There are many sources of environmental lead that could cause traces of lead to be on your fingertips.

4. Contamination could have caused the experiment to falsely identify dishware as containing lead.

5. Many health problems could occur including neurological, reproductive, and digestive disorders.

18. GLITTER AS TRACE EVIDENCE

Idea for class discussion: Ask students to make a list of items that might be found at a crime scene and used by investigators to help solve the crime. If glitter does not appear in their list, introduce it and ask whether or not it might be useful.

Notes to the teacher: Collect several types of glitter, preferably from different sources.

Analysis

1. small pieces of materials found at crime scenes such as hair, fiber, and soil

2. Answers will vary. Glitter is nearly invisible, easily transferred and easily collected. Although each piece of glitter is not unique, there are different types of glitter, which helps characterize a sample found at a crime scene.

3. Answers will vary but could include chemical tests and color analysis.

4. Answers will vary. Glitter has been used in some cases to link a suspect to a crime scene because not all glitter is the same.

19. RATE OF COOLING

Idea for class discussion: Discuss normal body temperature and ask students to speculate about how body temperature changes after death.

Analysis

1. Answers will vary. A small body cools faster because it has more surface area per volume.

2. Answers will vary. A body cools faster in water because water is a good medium for conducting heat away from the body.

3. Answers will vary. Clothing can insulate the body and slow cooling.

4. Answers will vary. Wind speeds cooling because it conducts heat away from the body.

5. Answers will vary.

20. CROSS SECTION OF TEXTILE FIBERS

Idea for class discussion: Discuss the concepts of cross sections and longitudinal sections.

Notes to the teacher: Use synthetic fibers so that students can see a variety of cross section shapes. Remind students to make extremely thin slices of paraffin when they are preparing their slides. Not all of the fibers in one slice will show a good cross section view, but some will. Encourage students to examine all of the fibers on the slide. The "crime scene" fiber should be the same as one of the unknown fibers.

Analysis

1. Fibers are very small and easily transferred between individuals.

2. Answers will vary. Fibers probably showed a variety of shapes, depending on their origins.

3. Wool and cotton are natural fibers that always have the same shape. They are not unique and cannot be traced back to one source.

4. Answers will vary depending on experimental results.

5. Cross sections shapes can help characterize fibers so that can be used as evidence that two individuals were associated in some way.

Glossary

adsorption attraction of gases or liquids to a solid material

algor mortis reduction of body temperature after death

analytes the components of a mixture that are to be separated during chromatography

autopsy examination of a body after death to help explain cause and manner of death

buoyant able to rise or float in air or in a liquid

capillary action the natural, upward movement of liquids, like the upward flow of water through fibers or in a tube

catalase enzyme that speeds up the breakdown of hydrogen peroxide into water and oxygen gas

cellulose strong, fibrous carbohydrate that forms the walls of plant cells

chromatography technique used to separate the components of a mixture by dissolving the mixture in a mobile phase that is passed over a stationary phase

cohesive relating to the force of attraction between molecules of the same type

decedent person who has died

density the mass of an object per unit volume

dental stone gypsum product that when mixed with water can be used to make casts and is used in dentistry to make impressions of teeth

DNA fingerprint unique pattern of an individual's DNA that can be used in forensic science as an accurate form of identification

effluent solvent that carries the analytes during chromatography; also known as the mobile phase

emission spectrum light emitted from a substance that is separated into its wavelengths

enzyme chemical in living things that speeds up or slows down reactions

gel electrophoresis technique used to separate the components of a protein or a nucleic acid by the movement of those components through a gel in an electrically charged field

glycogen stored form of glucose located in muscle and liver tissues of animals

half-life the time it takes for one-half of the atoms of a radioactive substance to decay

hemoglobin protein in blood that binds to and carries oxygen

hyoid bone U-shaped bone in the anterior portion of the neck to which muscles of the tongue are attached

indicator chemical used to detect the presence of acid or base

ion atom or molecule that is positively or negatively charged

ionic relating to ions; particles that carry positive or negative charges

isotopes atoms with the same number of protons but different numbers of neutrons

latent present but not visible

lividity characteristic discoloration of the skin of a descendant; also known as *livor mortis*

mass   the amount of matter in a material

mitochondria   organelle within a cell that converts glucose into a usable form of energy

nucleotide   subunit of DNA or RNA made up of a nitrogenous base, a phosphate group, and a sugar

organelle   membrane-bound structure within a cell that has a specialized function

oxidation-reduction reaction   chemical reaction in which the oxidized substance gives up electrons and the reduced substance gain electrons

oxidize   chemical reaction in which a material losses electrons to another substance, usually oxygen, resulting in the break down of a complex compound

pathologist   physician who studies disease and carries out microscopic analyses of tissues

polar   having positive and negatively charged poles or ends

post mortem interval   time between death and the discovery or examination of a body

probative value   evidence that helps establish the value of other evidence in a criminal case

product rule   formula to find how frequently a combination of traits occurs in a population

radioactive isotope   form of an atom with an unstable nucleus that breaks down by emitting energy and matter until a stable form is reached

rigor   rigidity of a body after death; also known as *rigor mortis*

specific gravity   ratio of the density of a material to the density of water

starch   stored form of glucose in plant cells

sublime   change in state from solid to gas without going through the liquid phase

surface tension   skin-like boundary between the surface of water and the air created by attractive forces between adjacent water molecules

trace evidence   small materials such as fibers, hairs, or soil particles found at a crime scene that might be used to link a suspect to the scene or to a victim

volume   the amount of space occupied by an object

Internet Resources

The World Wide Web is an invaluable source of information for students, teachers, and parents. The following list is intended to help you get started exploring educational sites that relate to the book. It is just a sample of the Web material that is available to you. All of these sites were accessible as of June 2008.

Educational Resources

Byrd, J. H. Forensic Entomology: Insects in Legal Investigations home page. Available online. URL: http://www.forensicentomology.com/index.html. Accessed June 5, 2008. Dr. Byrd describes insects found at crime scenes, discusses their life cycles, provides pictures, and explains how to catch and preserve them.

Chamakura, Reddy P. Reddy's Forensic Page. Available online. URL: http://www.forenslcpage.com/. Accessed June 5, 2008. Reddy is a forensic scientist who retired from the New York City Police Department. His site contains information on almost every topic in forensics.

Clemens, Daryl W. Crime and Clues, and Art and Science of Criminal Investigation. Available online. URL: http://www.crimeandclues.com/index.htm. Accessed June 5, 2008. Clemens in a crime scene technician whose site contains articles and links to forensic science resources.

Crime-Scene-Investigator. "Crime Scene Response," August 6, 2007. Available online. URL: http://www.crime-scene-investigator.net/csi-response.html. Accessed June 5, 2008. This Web site lists guidelines for crime scene investigators and contains articles by experts explaining how to treat and evaluate a crime scene, including Greg Dagnan's article listed below.

Dagnan, Greg. "Searching in Stages to Prevent Destruction of Evidence at Crime Scenes," crime-scene-investigator.net, March 17, 2007. Available online. URL: http://www.crime-scene-investigator.net/SearchingStages.html. Accessed August 13, 2008. Dagnan explains the correct way to examine a crime scene.

Federal Bureau of Investigation. "Kids Page." Available online. URL: http://www.fbi.gov/fbikids.htm. Accessed June 4, 2008. The FBI Kids Page presents information about the bureau's services and explains how cases are investigated.

FirearmsID.com, "An Introduction to Forensic Firearm Identification," 2007. Available online. URL: http://www.firearmsid.com/. Accessed June 5, 2008. This Web site contains pages that discuss types of firearms, rifling, ballistics, and other topics.

Forensic Dentistry Online. Available online. URL: http://www.forensicdentistryonline. org/forensichomepage.htm. Accessed June 5, 2008. Provided by Forensic Dental Services, Manchester Science, Park, UK, this Web site has links to resources on bite marks, identification through dental records, and other topics.

Forensic Science. "Let Evidence Reveal the Truth." Available online. URL: http:// library.thinkquest.org/04oct/00206/index1.htm. Accessed June 3, 2008. Prepared by a team of students with teacher coaches, this Web site is filled with interesting information and great pictures relating to forensic science.

Forensic Science Communications, Volume 10, Number 2, April 2008. Available online. URL: http://www.fbi.gov/hq/lab/fsc/current/index.htm. Accessed June 5, 2008. This newsletter presents articles related to forensic science and links to other resources.

Geradts, Zeno. Zeno's Forensic Page. Available online. URL: http://forensic.to/ forensic.html. Accessed on June 2, 2008. Geradts is a forensic scientist associated with the Netherlands Forensic Institute who supplies a variety of forensic information on his Web site.

Human Mitochondrial Genome Database. "Mitomap." Featured in *Science Netwatch*, Vol. 283, Issue 5407, Pages 1405–1592, March 5, 1999. Available online. URL: http://www.mitomap.org/. Accessed June 5, 2008. This Web site explains human mitochondrial DNA and shows a map of the genome.

Parkinson, Gregory A. "Stringing a Crime Scene to Determine Trajectories," *Journal of Forensic Identification*, Vol. 53, No. 4, July/August 2003. Available online. URL: http:// www.crime-scene-investigator.net/trajectories.html. Accessed June 5, 2008. This article explains the technique of stringing to show trajectories of bullets.

Ridges and Furrows home page. Available online. URL: http://ridgesandfurrows. homestead.com/. Accessed June 5, 2008. This Web page links to resources on fingerprints, including articles on the history of fingerprinting and the newest techniques in fingerprinting.

Will, Emily J. Forensic Document Examiner. Available online. URL: http://www.qdewill. com/. Accessed June 5, 2008. Will provides an overview of techniques used in examining questioned documents.

Index